HOW TO DEAL WITH A NARCISSISTIC PERSONALITY AND ESCAPE FROM A CODEPENDENT RELATIONSHIP

AN ULTIMATE RECOVERY USER GUIDE TO CURE CODEPENDENCY IN 45 DAYS

HELEN SHEPHERD

CONTENTS

Introduction   7

1. A Portrait of a Narcissist   13
2. What It's Like to Be in a Relationship with a Narcissist   41
3. The Codependency Trap   56
4. Face the Truth and Start Seeking Change   71
5. The Winning Guide to Communicating with a Narcissist   91
6. Healing from Codependency in 45 Days   101
7. When Is It Time to Say Goodbye   121

Conclusion   135
References   139

© **Copyright 2020 - All rights reserved.**

The content contained within this book may not be reproduced, duplicated or transmitted without direct written permission from the author or the publisher.

Under no circumstances will any blame or legal responsibility be held against the publisher, or author, for any damages, reparation, or monetary loss due to the information contained within this book, either directly or indirectly.

Legal Notice:

This book is copyright protected. It is only for personal use. You cannot amend, distribute, sell, use, quote or paraphrase any part, or the content within this book, without the consent of the author or publisher.

Disclaimer Notice:

Please note the information contained within this document is for educational and entertainment purposes only. All effort has been executed to present accurate, up to date, reliable, complete information. No warranties of any kind are declared or implied. Readers acknowledge that the author is not engaged in the rendering of legal, financial, medical or professional advice. The content within this book has been derived from various sources. Please consult a licensed professional before attempting any techniques outlined in this book.

By reading this document, the reader agrees that under no circumstances is the author responsible for any losses, direct or indirect, that are incurred as a result of the use of the information contained within this document, including, but not limited to, errors, omissions, or inaccuracies.

Are you Being Mind-Controlled by a Narcissist?
Find out if you are and learn how to escape it right now!

To receive your FREE guide visit the link:

https://helenbooks.activehosted.com/f/3

OR

INTRODUCTION

> "Narcissists are consumed with maintaining a shallow false self to others. They're emotionally crippled souls that are addicted to attention. Because of this they use a multitude of games, in order to receive adoration. Sadly, they are the most ungodly of God's creations because they don't show remorse for their actions, take steps to make amends or have empathy for others. They are morally bankrupt."
>
> — SHANNON L. ALDER

I know what it is like to live with a narcissist.

I have had personal experiences living with someone who has narcissistic tendencies. I can understand how it feels to live with a narcissist, especially if that person is close to you, like a romantic partner or a family member. Even if you have someone with narcissism in your social circle, such as a friend, acquaintance, or even a colleague, it can still be a mentally and physically exhausting venture to deal with them regularly.

Based on research conducted by the Diagnostic Statistical Manual of Mental Disorders (DSM-5) (Bree, 2018), about 6% of the population is diagnosed with Narcissistic Personality Disorder or NPD. That statistic might not alarm you. In fact, it might sound rather insignificant. But when you consider the fact that the population of the United States is around 327 million people, then based on the research, nearly 19 million people have NPD or NPD related characteristics. That's quite a large number, isn't it?

Because of the statistics, a large number of people are affected by narcissists and if you are one of them, then life can be quite a tiring journey. If you were to ponder upon the popular adage of "smelling the roses along the way," then let's say that in your life, you might not get the time to even notice that there are roses along the way. You might never have plenty of opportunities to experience life's beauties. You may feel drained frequently as you try and placate your partner, friend, acquaintance, or loved one. Your efforts to make him or her feel better, wanted or happy might go unnoticed or make things worse. At some point, your feelings of self-worth start taking punishments.

I am here to tell you that whatever you are feeling or going through is understandable and could even be justified. How do I know? Remember how I told you that I had lived with a narcissist?

That person is my mother.

Parents are often the child's first role model. Children look up to their parents for support, understanding, comfort, joy, and therapy. Parents become their children's advisor, confidant, best friend, and teacher. They play many roles and each role is based on trust and love. Which is why, the experiences I endured felt like a breach of trust. How can someone I love – and still love to this day – have caused so many emotional scars? After a traumatic childhood and numerous teenage difficulties, I set myself on a path to understanding narcissism. I wanted to not just find answers to my experiences, but methods to help people who are going through what I once did.

The events of my life guided me towards the field of psychology. I was honored with a master's degree from the University of California and extended my knowledge and experiences as a marriage and relationship therapist.

Over the years, I have worked with and helped many people who have been traumatized by narcissistic partners and significant others. Based on countless real-life experiences, I came up with my own unique approach to empower and help the victims of narcissists.

When I am not working with people, I am writing about personality disorders, codependent relationships, addiction, and abuse. It was while writing one of my articles that I realized I wanted to make my knowledge more accessible. I wanted to empower even more people and reach out to sufferers of narcissistic relationships better. As I was pondering these thoughts, the idea of publishing a book came to mind. I didn't think twice about it and dove headfirst into creating this book that you are reading now.

I decided to collate various high-profile studies and research performed on narcissism. And there are many.

For example, according to this study conducted by the University of Warsaw (Zajenkowski, Maciantowicz, Szymaniak &

Urban, 2018), narcissism can be placed into two categories, which form two extremes. On one side of the spectrum, you have grandiose narcissism, which is characterized by the overt presentation of feelings of entitlement and superiority. Grandiose narcissists are extraverts and they have the ability to blend well in social situations. Because of their grandiosity, they feel that they are somehow at a higher plane than the rest of us and are, therefore, subjected to special treatment. When I use the phrase "higher plane", I am not referring to anything metaphysical. Rather, I am talking about traits such as self-worth and social status.

On the other end of the spectrum, we have vulnerable narcissism. Because of the use of the word "vulnerable," you might think that this form of narcissism is quite mild. Perhaps such narcissists do not project self-aggrandizing qualities in an offensive manner. They are merely using self-importance as a means to defend themselves. However, reality presents another story altogether. Vulnerable narcissists have introversive tendencies, which means that they internalize their self-absorbedness. This is quite dangerous because when people are not obvious about their intentions, it is difficult to figure out what is going on in their minds. Additionally, vulnerable narcissists are highly sensitive to criticism. They feel their work has to be appreciated at all costs, regardless of the quality of work. They also have a high level of neuroticism, where they experience feelings such as worry, fear, depression, frustration, anger, anxiety, envy, jealousy, guilt, and loneliness. You might also have to provide them with reassurances constantly, as they tend to seek approval even when it is not required.

Two extreme forms of narcissism, yet both affect the people who come into contact with them.

But there is more to narcissism than merely classifying it. And I want to peel back the layers of understanding until you have a grasp on what it is and how you can deal with a narcissist in your life.

Let's dive further into the human mind.

1

A PORTRAIT OF A NARCISSIST

In Greek mythology, Narcissus was a hunter, born to the river god Cephissus and the nymph Liriope. Much was said about his beauty and many fell in love with him. Yet all he gave them in return was contempt and disdain. To him, others might as well be flies that needed to be chased away.

On one of his journeys through the woods, a nymph by the name of Echo fell in love with him. Narcissus spurned her advances and, in her despair,, Echo took her own life. As punishment, Nemesis, the goddess of revenge and retribution, beguiled him into a pool whose waters were crystal clear. When Narcissus approached the water, he spotted someone staring back at him. The person was so beautiful that Narcissus instantly fell in love, yet he was unaware at that point that the person was merely his reflection.

Upon discovering the truth, Narcissus realized that his love could not be a physical manifestation and the thought sent his mind spiraling down towards despair. Eventually, unable to carry his emotional burden, he committed suicide.

When we read the tale of Narcissus, we understand the lesson it is trying to impart to us, but we think that the events of the tale could not play out in real life. At least, not in the modern world. The myth was overdramatic after all!

Or is it?

Think about this for a moment. There are narcissists in today's world who disregard other people's attention in order to make themselves feel superior. It doesn't matter if someone wants to simply have a conversation with the narcissist; but they are ignored completely.

What about the part where Narcissus fell in love with himself so much so that he committed suicide? Well, perhaps that part is rather dramatic. However, when you take into perspective the character of a narcissist, then you realize that narcissistic behavior kills a person's character. All the empathy and compassion that they hold inside are slowly eliminated. While it might not be a literal suicide, narcissists end up performing a character suicide, where their goals merely become self-aggrandizing and self-centered.

A PORTRAIT OF A NARCISSIST | 15

Narcissists love themselves so much that they have "killed" positive traits such as compassion, love, and generosity.

So, What is Narcissistic Personality Disorder?

According to the Diagnostic and Statistical Manual of Mental Disorders (Huang et al., 2009), there are 10 types of personality disorders that are classified into three groups, or "clusters" as they are called.

Cluster A

This cluster features disorders that can be considered eccentric, bizarre, or odd. It includes the below:

- Paranoid Personality Disorder
- Schizotypal Personality Disorder
- Schizoid Personality Disorder

Cluster B

In this cluster, you will find those disorders that are deemed to be erratic or dramatic, such as the ones mentioned below:

- Antisocial Personality Disorder
- Histrionic Personality Disorder
- Narcissistic Personality Disorder
- Borderline Personality Disorder

Cluster C

Finally, we have cluster C disorders that are characterized by fearful and anxious traits. They include:

- Obsessive-compulsive Personality Disorder
- Dependent Personality Disorder
- Avoidant Personality Disorder

You might be wondering what the traits mentioned in each cluster represent. For example, what does it mean when a cluster is "eccentric, bizarre, or odd"? Let's take Cluster A. The traits mentioned in the cluster refer to personality disorders that describe behaviors that are marked by paranoia or unusual characteristics. For example, people with Schizoid Personality Disorder show a bizarre sense of apathy. They have limited emotional expressions, are highly secretive to the point that others might find it odd, and prefer a sheltered or solitary lifestyle.

Now let us examine Cluster B, where NPD resides. This cluster is marked by unpredictable, often erratic, behavior. Sometimes, people with these disorders present extreme volatility and project inappropriate behavior.

Cluster B does a good job of explaining NPD. Narcissists often display inappropriate behavior if they feel that the behavior can garner attention from people. They are unpredictable. At one point, they are charming and a few moments later, they can start displaying condescension to a high degree.

These clusters are useful in getting an overview of mental disorders. But each cluster by itself briefly touches upon a disorder. For example, Cluster B will help you understand what NPD is. But it does not delve into it. So, let's do that now.

When you hear the term Narcissistic Personality Disorder, then you are looking at a mental disorder. People who have the condition possess a sense of self that is distorted. They have concerning levels of self-importance, characterized by a neglect of the worth of others. People with NPD have an unhealthy obsession with power, prestige, and vanity. When their obsessions are not met, based on a degree of requirement that only the narcissist is aware of, then they express aggression and violence.

Their obsession compels them to seek out constant affection, admiration, and attention from others. However, once their demands are met, they are not satisfied. Instead, they increase their requirements, often at the cost of the emotional, mental, and sometimes physical well-being of the other person.

The Mark of Confidence

What is confidence?

You often see people claim that they are confident or someone remarks that they consider a person they know as confident.

Your confidence is a belief in yourself. You believe that you have the ability to meet life's challenges and overcome them, and act in a manner that portrays that belief. Now, just to be clear, when you are acting out your beliefs, it does not mean you walk with your chest up, your shoulders broad, and your head held high, thinking you're better than everyone else. Rather, it means that you have a realistic sense of your capabilities and are secure in the knowledge about yourself.

When you view yourself from a realistic standpoint, then you know the ups and downs of your character. This allows you to recognize your capabilities, character flaws, and other attributes. With such a realistic viewpoint, you can manage your confidence. You don't feel the need to exaggerate your accomplishments. Did you score just one goal in that soccer match with your friends? Then you will let everyone know it was just one goal. You won't try to embellish facts in order to enhance your standing in the eyes of others.

Other people, however, can become too overconfident to a point where it can be considered arrogance. When people fail to understand their limitations and capabilities, they find themselves failing at projects or unable to do certain tasks. The flipside to overconfidence is underconfidence, which can affect you negatively as well. If you have a lack of confidence, then you won't take risks in your relationships, work, or your life in general.

I would even say that confidence is acting well *in* your skin, not acting well *with* your skin.

You are proud of yourself and accept your faults because you want to work on them. You are open to constructive criticism, since you know that you are going to use them to better yourself. Additionally, confident people are altruistic. They do not just think about themselves but pay attention to the needs of others.

But in the case of a person with NPD, confidence takes on an unhealthy form.

Basically, narcissists do not have real confidence at all. They are not sure of themselves. This is why, as we had seen earlier, they seek admiration and confirmation from others. They wear a mask of confidence that they are able to make use of efficiently. Because of their mask, they are able to genuinely look confident, even though deep down, they have low self-esteem. With their false confidence, they are able to attract people into their lives. But over time, when their friends and acquaintances realize the true nature of the narcissists, they begin to fall out of a relationship with them.

The Guilt Factor

Because their levels of apathy are high, narcissists do not harbor any feelings of guilt. This becomes a problem for the victims, since they may try to explain away the narcissist's behavior. Surely, the victim may think, they must be the reason for the narcissist's behavior. Maybe it's something the victim did? Should they try and talk to the narcissist about it?

Many people have the ability to understand another person's state of emotions or mind. They are able to understand, feel, and share with others their values and motivations, their meaning of life, and what they are saying or trying to do. Essentially, people have the ability to have empathy. One of the best ways to describe empathy is to think of it as an ability. This ability allows people to form connections in order to have a shared emotional experience.

For a narcissist, such connections do not exist. You can't make them develop feelings of guilt. If you like, you can explain the situation in detail, but none of it will matter. They are detached from the situation.

This sense of detachment is apparent when narcissists exploit or manipulate others. They use a phenomenon called narcissistic supply, which is a psychological technique based on dependency and addiction. In this technique, the narcissists seek validation of special treatment, where he or she is given confirmation that they are "placed on a pedestal." They enjoy the feeling of people being dependent on them and they are addicted to the status that it gives them.

But how do narcissists achieve this? How do they manipulate others?

There are a few ways.

The All-Knowing

Some narcissists establish themselves – whether at work, home, or within a certain social situation – as the authority figures on certain subjects. It does not matter if they are well-versed or knowledgeable about the subject, they have to be the "know it all." They are frequent interrupters of conversations and hoarders of attention. This act of authority placement encourages them to become overly critical about others. Even when they are not correcting or criticizing you, they listen to what you have to say briefly before falling back to their original point, thereby nullifying your views – even though you may be right – and enhancing their stance on the subject.

The Controller

When people begin to allow narcissists to become a dominant figure in their lives, then the narcissists begin to subjugate and control those people. Some narcissists intentionally try to look for people who will be willing to give them that much dominance. Another variant of *The Controller* type of narcissism is *The Savior*. The narcissist will implant himself or herself as a person who "rescues" others. By doing so, they self-appoint themselves as people who are indispensable. They become the "saviors." Those they save begin to trust such narcissists will end up giving them the freedom to become dominant figures. The narcissists can then control the lives of the people they "rescued" in order to maintain the savior stance that they had established.

The Point Collector

Certain narcissists voluntarily pick up tasks or jobs regularly in order to be admired or feared. They don't do such work because they like it; they do it because they know they can attain a certain level of influence over the person or people they are doing the work for. It's like a point system; they do work to look better in the eyes of someone (almost like a twisted form of getting "brownie points"). The more "points" of trust they receive, the more they use that trust to control and manipulate people.

The Charmer

You might have come across certain people who use their charm to coerce or persuade others to do or give them something that they want. They do this even though the request is clearly unreasonable or one-sided. Often, the people receiving the request feel pressured into accepting the request. *The Charmer* influences people into doing what they want.

A narcissist may appear charming, but he or she is usually plotting something.

The Braggart

Have you ever been to the page of a social media influencer? You might have seen them posting about a charity they contributed to or a nice thing that they had done for somebody else? Or perhaps you might have noticed someone on LinkedIn bragging about how they love helping people get jobs and that others should do the same? These influencers and individuals engage in something called "humble-bragging."

Narcissists enjoy using "humble-bragging" as a tool of influence.

Of course, not all of them are humble. Some of them love name-dropping, showing off, overtly bragging, and even status boasting. They do this in the hopes of getting recognition, praise, or social media attention. They intentionally want others to be envious of what they do so that they can feel better about themselves.

The Negativity Creator

Some narcissists like to create a negative impression about themselves. They become persistently and deliberately confrontational, uncooperative, or difficult, even when it is unnecessary or unreasonable to be that way.

In their minds, reality takes on a negative form. They feel that they would rather get attention by being a thorn in other people's side than to be a nobody. There is a twisted form of perceived power that narcissists receive from being disliked and dreaded.

In some cases, the narcissist's low self-esteem goes on overdrive. When they start doing things that cause other people to have poor opinions of them, they instantly confirm their inner self-loathing. They use other people's reactions to prove that they are hopeless and worthless. Those negative feelings in-turn powers the narcissist's drive to acquire pity or sympathies, which they then use to manipulate those people.

The Hitchhiker

Some narcissists bask in the attention that someone else receives. They live through the lives of others because of their own unfulfilled hopes, dreams, and fantasies.

I once knew a parent who would dress up her daughter in doll-like outfits in an attempt to make her look "cute," even though her daughter had a "tomboyish" nature. The parent enjoyed the attention that she received through her daughter. When people complimented the daughter, it boosted the parent's self-worth. However, this harmed the growth and personality of the daughter. When parents themselves refuse to acknowledge their children's personalities and habits, they enable feelings of guilt. The children then start feeling as though their presentation and personality choices are something to be abhorred.

Everyone Is a Narcissist

The truth about narcissism is that it isn't a fixed trait, as we had seen before. What this means is that the trait exists on a spectrum, which means that we all have it to some degree. We all fall somewhere in the narcissism range.

In other words, we are all narcissists. But that is okay.

We all are probably guilty of doing something nice to someone, only to ask a favor in return. There must have been a moment in our lives, when we smiled and made small talk, only because we didn't want our request to be turned down by the other person. Or we might have done something – like talking over another person, stealing the spotlight or even showing we are better informed – to increase our chances of being visible or recognized in a situation. We are all guilty of doing few, some, or all of the things that narcissists do. So why aren't we all classified as having a disorder? What makes us different?

There are a few reasons:

We Have No Choice

In many situations, we might not have an alternative option.

For example, we realize that we have no choice but to ask a favor from someone. However, we don't want to simply take advantage of the person. We realize that we should try doing something in return. And so, we make small talk or try to do something small for them first. This shows a degree of concern or, in some cases, a sense of gratitude that we just want to express.

We Don't Like What We Do

We don't take pleasure in manipulating someone. We are racked with guilt about our actions. Some of us make an attempt to never repeat the act again. Others genuinely try to make up for their actions. For example, when we manipulate someone into doing something for us, we decide to return the favor in some other way.

We Apologize And Make Up For It

Some of us go as far as doing something genuinely nice for the person who helped us. We realize that it might not have been entirely fair to place the other person in such a position, and we take steps to show how apologetic we are.

Hold On! Is There a 'Good' Narcissism And a 'Bad' One?

There never really is a good and bad version of narcissism. There is just a harmless one and a harmful one.

When people have "harmless" narcissistic tendencies, then they are mildly self-centered at times. While this may sound like a negative trait, it is sometimes important to concern ourselves with our own welfare, ideas, goals, and thoughts. Narcissism flips a switch in our mind where we place ourselves before someone else.

But narcissism becomes harmful when it enters the realm of NPD.

Is There a Difference Between Narcissism And NPD?

Short answer – yes, there is.

But we need to know the long version if we hope to understand NPD. In recent years, there has been a rise in discussions surrounding the topic of narcissism. I have personally noticed people self-diagnosing their family, friends, and colleagues with narcissism. Despite the fact that narcissism is quite common among people, everyone claims to have a narcissist in their lives, especially at work where things can become quite heated. The term "narcissism" is easily thrown around to label someone.

When people group someone they know into a mental disorder simply because they dislike them, then it is not just unfair, but it is unethical. It is one thing to say something like "That person is just horrendous," but it is quite another to simply come out and say "That person is a narcissist. I think she has a disorder." In fact, when you or anyone else label people as having a mental disorder, then it serves to stigmatize people who actually do have a mental disorder. Alternatively, it could divert attention from the real problem. For example, people might actually have a severe case of depression, but then they suddenly find themselves being called narcissists. The situation can be harmful, since name-calling can worsen depression.

When I mention the different traits and the various forms of narcissists, bear in mind that while they are true, it does not mean that one can simply start grouping people into categories based on a few actions, words, traits, or habits.

According to the Diagnostic and Statistical Manual of Mental Disorders (Ambardar, 2018), an NPD can be diagnosed when the individual exhibits the following behaviors:

- An extreme need for gaining approval and receiving admiration from others.
- Presenting condescending behavior and having a sense of entitlement, where individuals see themselves as exceptional.
- A deficiency in the ability to recognize and understand the needs and feelings of others.
- Superficial connections and relationships.

- Extreme fluctuations in mood.

But it is one thing to know a list of traits and then quite another to go around looking at our close friends and family, hoping to find the traits in them. Do not diagnose someone as having NPD. Only a professional can truly make such diagnoses.

Common Types of Narcissists

You might not think that narcissism can be classified into many types. But using classification allows us to identify the way narcissism manifests in different people, since not everyone expresses themself the same way.

Narcissists may be part of the three main types:

- Classic
- Malignant
- Vulnerable

Classic

The classic case of NPD is the one that people can easily identify. The classic type includes people who are boastful about their accomplishments. In fact, many even make their accomplishments seem much bigger than they already are. If they had gone bungee jumping in an amusement park, then their version will replace the amusement park with a large cliff. When they finish a challenging task, they will focus on the challenge, making it seem more threatening and severe than it actually was. These narcissists can get bored easily when other people are not talking about them. In their state of boredom, they attempt to drag the attention back on them.

You might have come across a person having classic narcissism. There might have been a situation where you are talking about how you grew a beautiful garden in your house or finally finished the entire season of Game of Thrones in one sitting. Suddenly, the other person speaks up.

"Oh, yeah. I remember watching the first and second season in one go. You wouldn't believe how long I slept after that marathon."

All of a sudden, it seems as though the whole situation has turned into a competition, even when you weren't intending to compete with anyone. You merely wanted to have a nice conversation.

Malignant

This form of narcissism is one of the least common types. However, it is also considered as one of the most severe categories.

Malignant narcissism does not present itself with a fixed set of traits. To those who are not psychologists or mental health professionals, it becomes difficult to distinguish between NPD and malignant narcissism.

The one thing that sets this category apart from NPD is the fact that it includes people who have complete disregard for the emotions and feelings of others. Malignant narcissists deceive and manipulate people with a sense of satisfaction. They are not above emotionally or physically abusing someone to get what they want. Once they have committed their wrongdoings, they don't feel guilt or remorse.

A PORTRAIT OF A NARCISSIST | 29

Malignant narcissists do not have any sense of compassion. They enjoy emotionally attacking their partners.

Malignant narcissists have a sense of aggression that almost borders on psychopathy. However, aggression in and of itself cannot be diagnosed as a mental health issue. Only a professional might be able to connect the dots, linking the acts of aggression to the underlying narcissism that the person expresses.

One can even consider malignant narcissists as sadists since they enjoy the pain they inflict on others. They feel powerful and some are even sexually aroused by watching a non-consenting person receive physical or emotional pain.

In fact, one of the things that sets NPD apart from malignant narcissism is the amount of remorse felt by the individual. There is a small chance that people with NPD are capable of feeling a slight sense of remorse if they might have crossed a certain threshold. It makes them feel guilty, remorseful, or even uncomfortable. On the other hand, a malignant narcissist is devoid of such limitations.

If you have ever read or watched the classic thriller *Silence of The Lambs*, then you know that the character of Dr. Hannibal Lectar possesses high levels of malignant narcissism. He is utterly capable of mutilating his victims and deriving a certain satisfaction or sexual arousal from the act.

Vulnerable

Vulnerable narcissists are exemplary at putting up a facade. At first, they might seem so unobtrusive, which might make you feel comfortable around them. You might even appreciate the fact that they display immense modesty and low ego. You let your guard down and get to know them better. Soon, they start showing inattentiveness towards you. They begin to develop a victimization mentality. According to them, the world is out there only to make them suffer and that they are merely helpless bystanders. They become hypersensitive to critical comments. Even if you decide to give them advice because you sincerely want them to improve, they automatically assume that you are trying to cause them mental anguish. To them, you are probably envious of their success and are only trying to snatch their opportunities from them.

Vulnerable narcissism is marked by reticent behavior, extreme emotional reactions, and constant projection of helplessness. Because they are so emotional, they consider their emotions more important over others. For example, if a vulnerable narcissist is experiencing sadness and you are experiencing stress because of a long day at work, then they will disregard your emotional state of mind in order to get you to pay attention only to them. If you don't, then they think it means you dislike them or want to get rid of them.

Because of their victimization mentally, they believe that everything they do is perfect and if anyone thinks otherwise, then they are out to snatch their success from them.

Narcissism Subtypes

Apart from the types mentioned above, narcissism can also be expressed in a few subtypes.

Subtype 1: Overt And Covert Narcissism

Overt

An overt narcissist seeks to actively attract attention to himself or herself. It does not concern them in the slightest if the attention they receive is positive or negative. Overt narcissists are living proof of the statement "even bad publicity is good publicity." The only difference is that instead of publicity, they are seeking attention from other people.

It doesn't even matter if they are right or if they have rarely achieved anything noteworthy, they demand agreement and admiration. If they are not provided with what they seek, they respond with rage and impatience. Some of them even resort to violence.

If they cannot get things through violence, then they use flattery and charm. They are even capable of falsifying intimacy in order to get what they want. The surprising part of their reactions is that they actually might give off, what might seem like, genuine emotions. You might become convinced that they actually care or like you. However, their actions can crumble easily if you challenge their superiority. You see, even when they are trying to fake intimacy, they like to have the superior position. They consider other people as their "underlings," even people they seem to care so much about.

If you try to take away their sense of control, they can denigrate, mock, or ridicule you to regain their position. Other forms of narcissism can be classified under the overt category as well. For example, classic narcissists are overt. They don't try to hide their actions or use subtle moves.

Covert

Also known as a closet narcissist, a covert narcissist behaves in a passive-aggressive manner in order to get what they want. They might withhold information if they think they can use it against you in the future. When they take actions or employ words, they are insensitive to the feelings of others.

You might also catch them acting smug. They like to, as the expression goes, "rub it in the face" when they have done something correctly or when they are in the right.

Because their actions are not as bold as overt narcissists, they like to exploit people with caretaker personalities. Anyone with a caretaker personality places the welfare of others over his or her own. When narcissists come across such individuals, they use every trick in their book to latch on to the kindness and compassion of such individuals. Some covert narcissists are even capable of crying on cue or performing other self-pitying acts.

Their main weapon is their victimization mentality and they will make use of it to its full potential.

Someone who is a vulnerable narcissist is part of the covert narcissism category.

But what about malignant narcissism? Does it fall into a special category of its own? When someone is a malignant narcissist, then he or she can be overt or covert. In most cases, they can switch between the two subtypes, depending on their actions and how they choose to manipulate someone.

Subtype 2: Somatic And Cerebral

Somatic

These are the narcissists who enjoy taking selfies obsessively. They are willing to do anything to look good. They spend time at the gym or they are constantly hoarding makeup.

It is important to note that not everyone who goes to the gym or who uses makeup are part of this category. Quite far from it actually. I like to work out too and I enjoy regular exercises.

However, we are only referring to narcissists in this category. For example, there are some people who possess a six pack and arms that look like they can deflect bullets. When they see someone who is skinnier or chubbier than them working hard to build their body, they scoff at the person. They give a mocking smile or maybe even say something hurtful. Most people choose to encourage others in the gym, boosting their confidence and helping them reach their goals. But not narcissists. They like to bring others down so that they look good.

You might have noticed social media influencers who are constantly asking their followers for likes and comments, even when such likes and comments are not necessary. Instead of trying to communicate with their audience and create more content that their audience enjoys, they merely choose to take advantage of the fact that their followers are eager to see their next content.

Some people only live for attention and their social media attention.

Cerebral

These are the know-it-alls. They are the experts, even though they don't have an expert's degree or qualification. They consider themselves as the most intelligent person in the room.

If you have ever been on YouTube in the past year, then chances are that you might have stumbled across a video where somebody is trying to sell you a get-rich-quick mentorship program. For all intents and purposes, the person just wants your money and the whole thing is just a scam. But notice how they project themselves as the leaders of their subject. You might notice some people who are as young as 25 promoting themselves as "gurus."

A surgeon requires three years of undergraduate study, then has to focus on another three years in medical school before finally entering surgical residency. During the residency, he or she will spend another three or more years honing their craft. Only then are they even qualified to recognize themselves as experts in their fields. Now think about a situation involving a self-help guru. How can someone with barely even five years of experience in the business field be able to give you advice on how you can earn more money?

This is the case with most narcissists belonging to the cerebral category; they don't necessarily have the expertise. However, they would like to make you believe that they do.

Vulnerable narcissists are part of the cerebral category because they are often projecting themselves as perfectionists. It is not that they like to complete the job perfectly, merely that they believe they are perfect even when they produce poor results.

Other Special Types of Narcissists

Inverted

As more and more research was conducted on narcissism (The Narcissistic Life, 2014), special types were uncovered. One of those special types is inverted narcissism.

Inverted narcissists are also called codependents. This is because they use other people to receive their emotional gratification. They usually project themselves as subservient, demanding, or needy. They are constantly afraid of being abandoned. Even if their partner showers them with attention and love, these narcissists engage in immature behavior in order to gain more attention or become clingy. Most of the time, they like to pretend to be the victim, often pushing their partners or close friends to feel guilty about their situation.

But most importantly, inverted narcissists attach themselves to other narcissists. Because they can easily become subservient, they are accepting of the fact that they have to serve the needs of a narcissist. Some of them might even enter a relationship that is wrought with emotional or physical abuse. However, they continue to remain in the relationship because they cannot bear the idea of being abandoned.

Sadistic

Sadism is a psychosexual disorder where the perpetrator of the abuse, control, or pain is aiming to gratify his or her sexual urges through the actions inflicted on the victim.

The book and movie *Fifty Shades of Gray* depicts the kind of sadistic acts someone is capable of in order to derive sexual gratification. While many people enjoyed the book and film as a romantic plot about someone focusing on the power of love to improve themselves, the reality is much starker. However, it should be noted that the form of sadism depicted in the book and movie cannot be easily classified as a mental disorder.

Real sadists don't feel love or other emotions. They are ruthless in their quest to gain sexual satisfaction.

Remember that people display sadism even though they are unaware of it. You might get a rush when your favorite boxer gets the knockout punch. You feel invigorated by shooting someone at a paintball game. Action movies depicting the good guys inflicting violence on the bad guys may be your thing. In all of the above situations, you are taking pleasure from acts of cruelty. However, you or many other people like you do not have a mental disorder. You are not hoping someone really gets hurt or kills someone else. Additionally, you are not going to emulate the things you see on TV or read in a book on someone else just because you "felt like it."

However, sadists are those who are not above taking genuine pleasure in watching someone get hurt. Some narcissists, especially the malignant types, have a gleeful approach to inflicting pain and violence on others. In many cases, they don't need a justifiable reason to do what they do. They just like what they do. To them, inflicting pain could very well be something that feels like taking a walk down the beach.

Knowing about the different kinds of narcissism makes you wonder how someone could have all those traits. Were they born with it? What could cause them to become the person they are today? Is there an age-specific trait that results in narcissism?

Causes of Narcissism

The mind is a complex place. One cannot easily pinpoint the cause of a mental disorder because they may not have all the facts before them. For example, if you ask a psychopath what happened in his or her life, then the person might talk about past trauma. But did those traumas really cause the person to become psychopathic? Also, is the psychopath really telling the truth? Furthermore, is there a memory they are blocking, which could explain why they are psychopaths?

Since the mind is an intangible presence along with thoughts, memories, ideas, and dreams, it is not easy to test it or consider certain research results as facts. You don't have any tangible evidence to support your conclusions.

Which is why, the exact cause of NPD is usually shrouded in mystery.

However, here are some of the reasons that could lead to narcissism.

Upbringing

The individual's upbringing can play a major role in their narcissistic qualities. When parents are insensitive to the troubles of their children, the children themselves won't feel seen or heard. Their feelings will be ignored, often making the children feel like their parents don't care about them. The parents might treat the children like an accessory that they have to take care of, rather than people who are at a sensitive stage in their lives. In many cases, the parents value their children when they do something, rather than for who they are. Children begin to suffer from pain and loneliness. Because of the indifference of their parents, they might even hesitate to speak out, for fear of repercussions. All of the emotions that they bottle up inside causes them to develop negative emotions towards others, which in turn results in a negative outlook on life. They become detached from feelings of empathy, compassion, and kindness.

Genetics

This is a field that is still being studied by many researchers and medical professionals. According to one study (Luo, Cai & Song, 2014), there is a chance that a certain gene can cause narcissism to manifest itself in a person. In other words, narcissism can be an inherited trait.

However, it is important to note that just because it can be inherited, it does not mean that it can grow to harmful levels without other causes, such as the environment and upbringing. Merely saying that a person's genes caused him or her to become psychotically narcissist is a false diagnosis.

Neurobiological

A team of German scientists examined the brains of narcissists and noticed that half of the people in their study had a thin cerebral cortex (Chow, 2013), which is the part of the brain that is responsible for self-control, self-awareness, and self-determination. This means that narcissists are less aware of the effects of their actions. For example, if you are self-aware, then you are able to refrain from saying something hurtful to someone else. Or even if you do something harmful, you feel regret or guilt. In the case of a narcissist, their brains are not able to properly process their actions.

There are many reasons for the thinning of the brain. Usually, age plays an important role, but that is a natural process that occurs over a long period of time. It does not always explain narcissism in younger people. Other causes could include stroke and brain injuries.

Trauma And Abuse

When individuals are subject to trauma over a long period of time or intense trauma over a short period, then they develop what is known as trauma-associated narcissistic symptoms, or TANS for short.

Some narcissists might have faced trauma as children.

People with TANS begin to see the world differently. For example, if they received trauma from a woman in their life, then they aim to avoid such trauma in the future from other women.

They can become manipulative, cold, and remorseless in the way they treat women.

Abuse victims are also prone to this behavior. Usually, they project their negative emotions and feelings towards a particular demographic or group of people. However, that may not always be the case. Some abuse victims show narcissistic traits towards practically everyone they encounter in their lives, regardless of their age, gender, race or other characterizations.

Oversensitivity

Some people are really sensitive. And that is okay. They have a lot of emotional depth or they might not have people in their lives to encourage them to be more confident and sure of themselves. Either way, their sensitivity can cause mental and emotional damage to them, even for the most trivial of reasons.

When a certain threshold is reached, they become aggressive in order to prevent their emotions and feelings from being affected more. They begin to manipulate people, pretend to be victims, try to attract sympathy, and use the relationships they have to gain something.

Eventually, their oversensitivity can force them to become narcissists.

Not all oversensitive people become narcissists. Many just take on a shy persona. Others begin to work on their behavior to become more confident. So, the next time you come across a person who is sensitive, don't avoid them because you think that they might turn into narcissists. Reach out to them. Accept them for who they are. We could all do with a bit of love, compassion, and understanding in this world.

2

WHAT IT'S LIKE TO BE IN A RELATIONSHIP WITH A NARCISSIST

Being in a relationship with a narcissist or having a narcissist in the family, friend group, or social circle can be traumatizing.

After all, you have to see them almost every day. In some cases, you can choose to cut ties with the person, but in other cases, you might not have that freedom.

In many other cases, people don't want to "give up" on the narcissist because they feel guilty that they might be abandoning the person in a time of need. Unbeknownst to them, the narcissist might be aware of their intentions and might be manipulating them.

It is a complicated situation to be part of and not easy to deal with. Which is why it helps if you have more knowledge about what it is like to be in a relationship with a narcissist.

The Beginning

In the beginning, the relationship is going to feel special. You might as well call in Hollywood studios, because you have a romantic story in the making that you feel could rake in at least a million dollars at the Valentine's Day box office. Things are special. The romantic dinners. The special treatment. The sudden showcases of love. All of those actions will make you feel like you are living in a dream.

Until you realize that it might as well have been a dream, since most of what you experienced was part of an elaborate plan by a narcissist to lull you into a false sense of security.

Some narcissists even employ a technique called "love bombing," where they constantly send you texts, surprise you with presents, or show affection at almost every opportunity they get.

Eventually, when the charm and magnetism begins to devolve, you notice the true nature of a narcissist.

Lack of Empathy

Narcissists lack empathy, which means that their partners will rarely feel seen, appreciated or understood.

Narcissists are comfortable ignoring someone.

You could compliment a narcissist and they will enjoy the attention. But don't expect anything in return, even if you do something special for the person. In fact, if people with NPD do not receive compliments, then they will start fishing for it. They might pretend to do something nice and when you compliment them, they will stop doing it until they require their next compliment fix.

Narcissists also don't deal with emotions that have to do with someone else. They don't care if you had a bad day at work, scuffle with your friends, or fight with your parents. You might mention the situation to them and they might turn the attention back to themselves. For example, you might talk about how you had a truly stressful day and they might respond with, "Oh that's bad. Guess what? Today I had so many tasks to take care of. But I actually got them done. I feel like there is a promotion in the near future."

All of a sudden, it is not about your stressful day. It is about what they did at work. Their inability to empathize, or even show a small amount of sympathy, is why some of them don't remain in relationships for long or even if they do, their partners are being manipulated into staying in the relationship.

Gaslighting

In gaslighting, the manipulator is trying to get someone to question their own perceptions, memories, or reality. Usually, the manipulator gaslights the person slowly. That way, the victim does not feel like he or she is being manipulated or realize how much they have been brainwashed into thinking in a particular manner.

How does a narcissist gaslight?

For one, they tell blatant lies. In fact, even if you know what they are saying is a lie or call them out on it, they do it anyway. Why?

Because they are establishing some kind of foundation for future actions.

They will lie blatantly and make you question them at every turn. Then they will throw in some truth. When you question them, they will reveal the truth, making you feel guilty about doubting them. Soon enough, you won't be doubting them anymore.

You will begin to doubt yourself.

They even start using your friends and people close to you as ammunition. For example, you might say that things are stressful to you because you have to not only take care of projects but also take care of your kids. They will then question you and ask why you had kids in the first place if you were not ready. Such questions will make you wonder about your decisions. You will not hate your kids or blame them, but you will begin to blame yourself for bringing your kids into a world where you cannot take care of them properly. And once you start having such negative thoughts, you will be shocked that you had them in the first place. Are you such a cold-hearted person to harbor such feelings? Are you secretly a monster?

See what I mean? All of a sudden, you are doubting your thoughts and your personality. You forgot that the entire reason your train of thoughts took on such a dark turn is because of the narcissist. Yet you are not a cold and emotionless person. You are someone who feels guilty about doing something. To you, thinking negative thoughts about your family or friends fills you with remorse.

Now you might wonder how it is that you are not prepared for gaslighting. Here is the most insidious thing about the tactic; it is done slowly and over a long duration. It's a small lie here. A manipulation there. Perhaps the occasional snide comment. Eventually, you become worn out. You lower your mental defenses and are left open to any form of manipulation.

I can tell you that even the brightest and most intelligent people become victims of gaslighting.

Think of the analogy of the frog in the frying pan. If you gradually turn on the heat, the frog won't realize what is happening to it until it is too late.

Even if you start doubting the narcissist, they will throw in the occasional nice gesture or compliment to confuse you.

Now you might wonder, how will the narcissist know that you doubt them? It is not like they can read your mind, right?

Actually, they know what you are thinking about them because you tell them. You are a person who genuinely cares. You are filled with love and compassion. When it comes to it, you don't hide your feelings and use them to your advantage. You like to talk about the situation openly and come to a positive conclusion. That is, you, a person with empathy, kindness, and the ability to care wholeheartedly.

What happens when you approach a narcissist with your doubts or thoughts? They change their stance. All of a sudden, they act as though they have understood you. But that is just the pretense for what is to come; more gaslighting.

No Apologies

One of the things you might notice about narcissists is that they will not apologize. Even when you catch them in the act of doing something wrong or have proof to show their wrongdoings, they will never even remotely feel sorry.

Here, I am going to inject social media influencers again. Quite frankly, I enjoy the content created by many social media influencers. But here is where things enter the gray area. You might have noticed some influencers manipulate their audience or do something that breaks the trust of their followers. They immediately create an "apology video" to explain their actions and redeem themselves in the eyes of their followers.

However, many of the apology videos are devoid of the one content they are made for; the apology itself. Instead, the influencer will use reasons to justify their actions, talk about another unrelated matter in their life (basically throw in a straw man argument), or even talk about how things will be different in future content.

But where is the apology? Where is the sign that they feel bad about their actions?

Similarly, you cannot expect a narcissist to not feel sorry for what they had done.

Lack of Boundaries

Many people have asked me if setting boundaries in a relationship is healthy or not. There are a lot of misconceptions surrounding boundaries. Many people feel that their relationships should be based on trust and where trust is involved, boundaries are absent. But to better understand this concept, let us look at some healthy and unhealthy aspects in a relationship:

Healthy	Unhealthy
You are able to feel responsible for your own happiness	You are constantly feeling as though you are incomplete without your partner
You are allowed to have friendships outside your relationship	You are only relying on your partner for joy and companionship
You and your partner encourage open and honest forms of communication	There is a level of manipulation involved or one or both of you play games with the other
You respect your partner's differences	You or your partner envies the unique qualities of the other person
You honestly ask for what you would like	You feel like you are unable to express what you want, like or dislike

Sometimes, we feel that boundaries are unimportant or even unnecessary. After all, our partners should be able to easily tell what we want and need. Boundaries can remove the feelings of being special or ruin the relationship.

In reality, every healthy relationship has boundaries. For example, you are able to tell your partner that when you are working at home, you should not be disturbed unless there is an emergency. In a healthy relationship, your partner will respect and understand that.

In an unhealthy relationship, your partner might constantly interrupt you for attention. He or she might make you feel guilty about working hard, telling you that you pay more attention to work than family.

Such actions are harmful and they affect the relationship heavily. A narcissist likes it when there are no boundaries. That way, he or she will constantly break promises, disrespect your sexual discomforts and preferences, and do things that you might not approve of. They might take money without asking for your permission and spend it on trivial things. When you tell them about something that is important to you, they forget about it quickly or worse, they won't care about it.

Worst of all, when they are guilty of breaking boundaries, they somehow manipulate the situation to make you feel like you were the reason they committed their actions.

Unreasonable Entitlement

What exactly is entitlement? These days, the word is thrown around so casually to talk about someone or describe a complete stranger. Yet it seems as though some people do not fully understand its meaning.

Entitlement refers to an unreasonable expectation where a person should receive special or automatic compliance simply because he or she made such expectations or because of who they are.

So how does a narcissist display entitlement? For example, narcissists might take umbrage at the fact that someone else got the attention that they deserved. Or they might complain about the fact that you use terms of endearment for someone else other than them and question why they don't have similar or better terms. Some narcissists may even feel entitled to your money, which connects to their ability to break boundaries with your financial assets. Others use your relationship or their position as your partner to have sex with you whenever they want, even when you are not in the frame of mind for sex. When it comes to your needs, they spur your sexual advances if they are not interested. In many cases, if you are having a good day but the narcissist had a bad one, they go out of their way to turn your day horrendous.

The irony of the situation is that narcissists act out in so many ways that they themselves might not tolerate from others. When asked about their actions, they will have a justification ready.

Manipulation And Guilt-Tripping

A manipulator uses verbal or nonverbal methods to induce guilt in a person over a long period of time. The manipulator does this in order to gain some kind of control over the victim. Because of this, guilt trips are a form of coercion method.

There are many ways that manipulators use guilt trips. For example, let's say that you were reversing your car out of a garage and accidentally bumped into a pillar. The narcissist will continue to point out your mistakes in the future. Every time you get into the car, he or she will subtly make you feel guilty by asking, "Are you sure you can drive? I could reverse out of the spot for you" or "You are going to bump into something again. Let me do it."

Narcissists are good at guilt-tripping their partners.

Now it is understandable if the person is concerned and they are genuinely displaying that concern. So how can you differentiate between an act of worry and one that involves manipulative tendencies? Well, you look at the timing of the response.

When people are concerned, they only act worried when the situation repeats itself. A narcissist, on the other hand, will remind you of the incident even when it is not required. For example, you could be out shopping with your partner and suddenly, the conversation of your mistake might make an appearance. Or perhaps you both are watching a movie when the narcissist might make a quip about how the person in the movie is driving better than you are.

Guilt trips are fairly common among family members. But they are usually benign. We understand the reasons for our family members doing what they do. Usually, we understand that they are coming from a good place. With a manipulator, we don't know why they commit certain actions or choose to send you on a guilt trip.

Guilt-tripping is dangerous when you decide to end a relationship with a narcissist. They will manipulate the situation, and your emotional state, to make you feel guilty of even the smallest of things in order to make you stay. In some cases, the manipulator might realize that they might not find another person to treat them the way their current partners are doing. They fear losing all the attention they had been getting so far. Some narcissists – especially those who are prone to acts of violence, whether physical or verbal – lash out at their partners. Other narcissists become unresponsive.

Not responding properly has its own effect on the victim. Think about this situation. You are talking to a child but he or she is staying silent, perhaps even pouting. You immediately know that you might have done something to offend the child in some capacity. You try to talk to them and perhaps change the situation. It is the same with a narcissist. When they stay silent or unresponsive and the victim responds to that silence, it does not mean that the victim is gullible, it just means that the victim experiences intense guilt, as though they have done something to cause offense. In quite a few cases, the victims try to explain themselves. The more explanations they provide, the more ammunition the narcissist has to use on the victim.

Isolation

Because narcissists cannot stand the fact that you can provide someone else – such as your family or friend – attention, they try to isolate you from meaningful relationships.

They might manipulate you into thinking that your family or friends are harboring ill-will towards you. Since you trust the manipulator, you don't question his or her intentions. You feel like he or she might be telling the truth. After all, they have your best interests at heart. Don't they?

In the absence of other relationships, you begin to depend on the narcissist for companionship. In fact, they might just become your only form of companionship. Remember how, when we were discussing the difference between a healthy and an unhealthy relationship, we mentioned what could cause relationships to be unhealthy? You might have come across this point: *you are only relying on your partner for joy and companionship.*

Here is what happens when you start to have only a person for comfort or joy; you begin to experience a sense of loneliness. You won't understand where the feeling comes from or what causes it. After all, you remind yourself that you have a remarkable and caring person in your life. However, your mind subconsciously knows that you were surrounded by friends and family. Your conscious mind, on the other hand, has accepted the new reality you are in and built defenses around itself to ward off any thoughts that might change your perception. Your subconscious mind is more persistent. It tries to send in signals every now and then in the form of emotions.

Eventually, you start maintaining your relationship at a shallow level, devoid of meaningful interactions, emotions, and experiences. You begin to justify your position. There is a sense of guilt that flows through when you even begin to so much as doubt your present situation. Sometimes, your doubt makes you ask yourself how you could even be so callous and selfish.

The more you self-blame, the more leverage the narcissist has.

Extreme Jealousy

Because some narcissists must have experienced an emotional situation in their lives, where they were humiliated, went unnoticed for long periods of time, or subjugated at an important stage in their life, they often seek to replace what they had lost. The issue of recognition is fraught with confused and resentful feelings, thoughts, and memories.

The mind of a narcissist is highly binary. It functions as a sequence of ones and zeros or from a psychological perspective, it is all or nothing for them. Your success or good feelings are a reflection of them, but not in the way that you might think. They feel that because you succeeded, it automatically means that they failed. It does not matter if they are connected to the reason for your success. All that matters is that you did or received something and they didn't.

When you start receiving attention for your work or actions, then they see the situation as a missed opportunity for themselves to gain some attention, respect, or love. Most people rightly and rationally believe that there is enough respect, attention, and love to go around for everybody. Narcissists, on the other end, believe that only a certain few individuals get recognized. And those few individuals have to be them.

Furthermore, when you succeed, your friends and family who care about you are genuinely happy for you because they don't see your success as a challenge to them. They understand your hard work, dedication, and all the other efforts you put into the work. Narcissists, on the other hand, often chalk your success to luck.

Sadly, no amount of convincing can change a narcissist's mind.

Intermittent Attention

A narcissist gives you attention under certain conditions or if they have a certain mood. These conditions should be met if you are "deserving" of their attention. Often, you don't know what these conditions are because they keep changing. One moment, you are doing everything possible to appease a narcissist's mood and the next second, you are left feeling guilty of doing the "right" thing.

This situation becomes a tiring experience. Think of an action movie with a really long chase sequence. At first, you are entertained and are at the edge of your seat. Soon, you begin to think to yourself; is this ever going to end? It is the same with a narcissist. You keep going around in circles, chasing their requirements until you are left emotionally exhausted.

Being emotionally drained around narcissists means that they take advantage of you. Which means you cannot catch a break at all. You are constantly on edge. This situation is not just emotionally harmful to you, but physically as well. When you are constantly tense, then your body's fight-or-flight reactions are on full alert. Your body floods your system with hormones such as cortisol. One of the features of cortisol is that it fills your system with glucose. Imagine if your blood is constantly pumped with glucose. Yes, it can be quite harmful to your health.

The Change Starts With Knowledge

Most people don't know that they are under the influence of a narcissist.

Imagine that you have joined a workplace where you have to work six days a week. Initially, you might feel a sense of rebelliousness within you. After all, six-day work weeks was not what you had in mind initially. However, over time you become comfortable with the situation. You are so used to six-day work weeks that you have completely forgotten about your original plan.

When you are with a narcissist, you might feel uncomfortable about their manipulative methods or feel like you would like to talk to them about it. As time passes by, you get used to the situation. Living with a narcissist becomes the new norm. Pretty soon, you can't imagine life without the narcissistic person.

It is difficult to break out of the spell you fall under. After all, narcissists are good at manipulating the people around them.

This is why it is important to equip yourself with knowledge. The more knowledge you have, the more you are able to pierce the veil of manipulation, lies, and deceit that the narcissist creates to keep you under his or her control.

While we are on the subject of knowledge, let us look at another important factor that you should be aware of; codependency.

3

THE CODEPENDENCY TRAP

Without a doubt, codependency creates unhealthy relationships and marriages. Codependency has, what many would like to say, as the positive side and the negative side. But the real kicker is this; even the positive side is destructive. Now, when I use the term positive side, I am not saying that there is any benefit to the victim. Rather, the "positive side" refers to the fact that victims who experience that side begin to mistake it for real love before becoming ensnared in the trap. In other words, victims begin to develop "positive" feelings.

However, I have my own way of labeling codependency. From my perspective, I don't like to use the terms negative side and positive side. We should truly address them as the negative sides and the false-positive sides.

Relationships with narcissists are often described as codependent and there's a simple reason why. One definition of codependency is feeling responsible for other people's feelings, problems, behaviors and life circumstances. Narcissists know how to utilize such feelings to their advantage, because their victims begin to feel responsible for them.

Let's take a further look at codependency.

What is Codependency?

Codependency is a situation where one person in the relationship – in this case, the victim of a narcissist – has to sacrifice his or her personal needs in order to satisfy the needs of the other person, who is the narcissist.

Codependency is characterized by certain traits.

As a person in a codependent relationship, you will find yourself doing some or all of the below:

- Being a perfectionist and fearing failure. You might not want to disappoint the narcissist you live with because you dislike their reactions.
- You won't be able to be critical. The narcissist becomes sensitive to criticism.
- The partner will be in constant denial of the fact that there are any personal problems. He or she might think that everything is going well.
- You will find yourself focusing on the needs of the other person excessively. There may be moments when you are able to focus on yourself, but those situations are too few and far in between.
- You might feel a sense of discomfort from asking help from others or receiving any outside attention since your whole world revolves around the narcissist.

As a victim, you will be afraid of asking for help for fear of the consequences.

- You might start feeling guilty about the suffering of your partner and you find yourself constantly taking responsibility while your partner does not take any responsibility for his or her actions.
- You are reluctant to share the truth about your situation to others. In many cases, people are even hesitant about trying to talk to someone about their situation.
- You might experience a sense of low self-esteem. Even if you were a confident person before, you might end up becoming someone who looks down on yourself.
- You begin to measure your self-worth based on how well you take care of the narcissist in the relationship. If you do not perform adequately, you begin to look down on yourself.
- Eventually, you start feeling as though you don't deserve happiness. You must have done something wrong. This could be karma. You were not smart enough. There are so many reasons that you employ to blame yourself.

What Does Codependency Look Like With a Narcissist

When you are living with a narcissist, whether that person is a romantic partner, a friend, a parent, or a flat mate, you will feel unappreciated or underappreciated, uncared for and unimportant. At the same time, you will find it very difficult or even impossible to leave. This type of relationship has codependent parameters that make it so difficult to decide what you're going to do. The reason is simple – the person who is emotionally destroying you on a regular basis is also the one who's building you up every now and again. You get emotionally attacked, and motivated. The fluctuations in your treatment are so confusing, you don't know where you stand with the narcissist.

Furthermore, codependency stifles the development of real feelings and love. Anything remotely resembling genuine emotions is crushed under the weight of manipulation and lies. Additionally, codependency can prevent a person from healing from past traumas. They are reminded of past mistakes repeatedly.

How does this happen? If you are caring for a narcissist, then you try to make up for the mistakes of the past, however minor they may be. You think that whatever happened in the past was a result of your actions and so you must do everything to prevent them from happening again. It could have been a situation where you might not have prepared a meal for the narcissist. The narcissist might have reacted negatively, perhaps even thrown a fit of rage. From that point onwards, you make it your life's mission to never forget another meal ever again.

A Real Life Example

For the purpose of confidentiality, I am going to withhold the names and true identities of the people I am talking about. However, I worked with a woman living in a codependent relationship. Her husband had an affair four years prior to the time I had come into contact with her.

After a while, the woman's entire focus began to zero in on her husband and making sure she was there for him. If her thoughts were not on her husband, they were angry at the relationship he had. She stopped focusing on other people, never paid attention to her own needs or requirements. Her thoughts are completely consumed mentally and emotionally by the presence of her husband.

On the other hand, her husband had long stopped respecting her or genuinely caring for her. He even feels stifled by all the attention and work that she does for him. But despite how the husband thought of the wife, she continues to take care of him. She focuses on his needs, his work, and his personal life. She found herself pondering many times whether he was happy or not.

Despite the advice she received from me, her friends, and even her own family, she refuses to acknowledge her situation. The fact of the matter is that she has become used to her new conditions. She can't get out of being stuck.

This above situation is fairly common among many victims who are in a codependent relationship. No matter what happens, a codependent will find a way to continue living in the relationship he or she is part of through all the trauma and pain.

Now it isn't entirely alien for people to forgive their partners for their past transgressions. Usually, it happens after a proper conversation and evaluation of the relationship. But continuing to suffer in silence without concern for self, all the while enduring emotional – and maybe physical – trauma and abuse, is not normal.

Other Ways Codependency Can Manifest

There are many ways that codependency can take place. In some cases, two people with dysfunctional personality traits coming together to mutually harm each other. When such people form relationships, they seem to fill a particular gap that the other one has. It could be attention, need, or even something as simple as sex. When they start depending on each other for small things, they begin to increase their demands. Before they know it, they are both in a codependent relationship. In many cases, each person feels that they are not going to be able to find a better relationship than the one they find themselves in.

Codependents think: Sure, things have their ups and downs, but what relationship doesn't right? Using such justifications, they continue to create a toxic environment for each other.

Codependency can also take place in perfectly normal relationships. When there are no clear boundaries, then people start to live unhealthily. For example, if you are not allowed to step outside with your friends or go visit your family, then you begin to depend on your partner exclusively. That situation alone can create codependency. In some cases, the person does not realize that he or she has become codependent.

Codependent relationships make you feel like you are trapped and there are few options left for you.

The Case of Passivity

Many people who fall into a codependent relationship are those who are passive and timid. They are drawn to the confidence of the narcissist.

Confident narcissists are able to draw people towards them. They have a magnetic personality and can say the right things at the right time.

Once a victim becomes part of the relationship, then he or she is subjected to manipulative behavior. But not a lot happens quickly. The pace of destructive behavior is slow. It starts with a few comments that the victim believes is true. After all, how can they question someone who is so sure of themselves? That person must surely have an incredible life experience or a vast repository of knowledge. Eventually, the comments turn to demands and then come the emotional, and sometimes even physical, abuses.

Narcissists can hide their true nature.

Codependents and narcissists both have an undefined or unrealistic sense of self. To some degree, they represent the opposite sides of the same coin and they're drawn to each other for that specific reason.

In other words, they project themselves on the other person. If the narcissist is doing well or is happy, then the codependent is satisfied. On the other end, if the codependent is subjugated and compliant, then the narcissist is happy. This situation becomes a cycle of destruction. Even if conflicts were to arise, neither party would do anything to break the cycle. In many cases, codependents forget that they had a better life before they met the narcissist. They feel that for as long as they can remember, the life they are leading with the manipulator is the one that they have always known.

A Sense of Denial

In the beginning, there is a denial of the fact that there is anything amiss.

Eventually, you might discover that your partner is hurt because they think you have been ignoring them for a long time or failed to keep their promises multiple times. But you cannot figure out why anything like that would happen. You would never blame the relationship. In order to make amends, you decide to redouble your efforts to be a partner, one who is caring and genuine.

You then start to imagine how the other person would feel about certain things. Based on your conclusions, you alter your behavior in order to accommodate their feelings.

In this situation, one person wants to be truly happy while the other is solely focused on making that person happy. There is a level of expectation that the demanding person wants from the willing person.

A situation of codependency has been created.

Slowly, a sense of resentment begins to build up inside the codependent. After all, what was once offered freely now seems to be demanded. More than that, the recipient wants whatever is given in bigger quantities. For example, if you are codependent in a friendship, then the time you had given to your friends suddenly doesn't feel enough. They ask you to spend even more time with them. In the beginning, guilt overtakes you and you relent to their request. After all, you should be a good friend. Over time, you realize that you are the one who likes to make things work while the efforts made by your friends are minimal.

You might process the relationship, but you would never conclude that you are codependent. If you admit that, you are officially declaring that your friend has been manipulating you. And that fact is a bitter pill to swallow.

Sometimes, people feel the frustration of the obligation placed on them and they try to withdraw from the relationship. But whether it is loyalty, love, respect, or responsibility, they are drawn back into the web of control.

If you are codependent, then it is understandable that you are trying to avoid breaking the relationship you respect and admire. You don't want to lose a good friend, a beloved family member, or a partner you have fallen head-over-heels for. However, what you have to understand is that there is an important factor in your relationships, without which nothing could work properly.

That factor is you.

You have to realize that if you are not feeling mentally or emotionally healthy in your relationship, then your mind is ripe for manipulative behavior. It is not easy to notice whether you are being manipulated by someone or not. After all, it's not as easy as looking at someone's brain and then clearly seeing, through examination, that they are narcissistic.

The brain weighs about three pounds and is the size of a cantaloupe. Somewhere, deep within its circuitry, lies the sequence that makes narcissists who they are. If you examined the brain of a narcissist, then you will not find one that is blue or has wavy designs spread across it. You are going to find the same lump of gray matter.

The only way you can find out whether you are being manipulated is by examining your own life. You need to start taking into account how much freedom you have for doing the things that you want. Do you feel confident that you have the freedom to attend to your needs and requirements? Are you guilt-tripped into doing something frequently? Have you gone out and made friends with people?

Step 1: Begin Practicing Self-Care

When you are part of a codependent relationship, then you might find yourself losing sight of your needs. You begin to alienate yourself and fill up your mental space with thoughts of others, whether they are your friends, family or loved one. That way, most of your time and energy has been distributed among other people, while you take the leftovers. In order to move forward and develop healthier relationships, you need to take time to explore yourself.

If you are already used to adhering to a routine that depends on the demands of other people, it is going to be difficult for you to break out of that routine. But do it slowly. Start by taking the time you would usually give someone else to explore your likes, dislikes, needs, desires, feelings, and thoughts. I encourage you to use a book or software to write down points about yourself. The problem with trying to remember things is that you might forget the points you came up with. When you forget them, it feels as though there aren't enough aspects of yourself worth remembering. However, when you write down in a book, you can simply pick up the book at a later date and remind yourself just how unique you are.

Step 2: Become Independent

Start doing things by yourself. For example, if you found satisfaction only by spending time with someone, then you should start finding joy in things that you do. It could be anything. You can start painting, watching Netflix and chilling, playing video games on that Playstation collecting dust, or simply picking up your outdoor photography hobby. Whatever you decide to do, you simply have to devote your attention to it.

Start doing the things that make you happy.

Once you are happy doing something, start doing it repeatedly. Make time for it every day. For example, between 7 PM to 10 PM, you are going to watch The Mandalorian TV series or one movie from the Marvel Cinematic Universe.

Now here is the challenge; there are going to be situations where your friend or loved one will begin to interrupt you. They see you enjoying something, and they think to themselves that if you have the time to focus on yourself, then you should be spending that time on them instead.

Here is the truth; you don't have the time for them. No, you have the time only for yourself. Unless there is an emergency, you are going to focus on your activity. It might be difficult at first. You are going to feel guilty about doing it. What is happening to my friend or family member? Should I check up on them right now and make sure they have everything they need? Maybe I could leave them a text?

You matter. If there is something that you need to take care of, do so before you sit down for your activity. You can arrange your "me-time" by taking into consideration all the activities and tasks you have to do for the day, such as going to work, cooking, or finishing chores. But try to plan some time for yourself when you know that no one can interrupt you easily.

Add more time for yourself if you can. The more independent you become, the faster you begin to break the spell of codependency.

Step 3: Evaluate Your Life Realistically

Once you have given yourself more independence, sit down and try to evaluate your life from a realistic perspective. Don't expect other people to fulfill you. Allow yourself to realize that you are happy because you choose to be happy and for who you are as a person.

Then list down the things where you notice someone placing unrealistic expectations on you. This step might be difficult because you might try to justify the intentions of people. But without trying to provide any explanations, start making your list and add as many instances of codependency you can find. Then try to find ways to deal with those situations. For example, is your friend making you hang out with him or her almost every day and is that affecting your life? Do you feel that you are constantly exhausted in the evenings and you have no time to breathe or simply relax?

Try to look for ways to take some time out for yourself. Then set aside some time for your friend, if you like. Don't feel guilty for saying "no."

Step 4: Practice Boundaries

Whenever there is codependency, there is a lack of boundaries. When you are spending most of your time worrying about other people, then you are paying less attention to the liberties other people take from you. After evaluating your life, you begin to notice the areas where people seem to take advantage of you. It could be your finances, where someone assumes that the money you have in your bank account or your wallet might as well be theirs. Or it could be your hard work, where you might be doing all the chores and they simply add to the pile without doing anything themselves.

Once you start setting up boundaries, you automatically start freeing up more time for yourself.

Once again, say "no" to people. If someone asks you to do something that you are not supposed to do, then reject the request with confidence. This confidence might be difficult to practice in the beginning. But that is okay. You will learn over time. The trick is to keep repeating the action until it becomes easy for you to employ.

Step 5: Deal With Your Past

Sometimes, your tendency to become part of a codependent relationship might be because of past trauma. You need to examine your past. Look for behaviors that might explain why you react the way that you do. Examine your family, situations of abuse or neglect, or other events that may play a huge role in preventing you from being comfortable with who you are.

It might be difficult to do it alone. If so, then seek out the help of a therapist. Remember that digging up things from your past may be painful. But it is important to put them to rest so that you can move on with your life.

Step 6: Reach Out To a Therapist

When things seem too difficult to handle, then don't try to attempt anything on your own. For example, if you feel extremely uncomfortable trying to dig up the past, then you don't have to do it alone. When you work with a therapist, then you have a professional who will be able to guide you in the right direction.

Therapy will help you get professional advice.

In fact, for any of the steps mentioned above, you don't have to do it alone if you are finding it increasingly stressful or difficult to do so.

There is no shame in seeking out a therapist. Many people feel that therapy is indicative of their weakness and inability to handle the situation themselves. I will tell you this right now; nobody can treat themselves effectively. As a friend, I urge you to not treat yourself. The consequences of something failing can be disastrous. It is okay to ask for help.

4

FACE THE TRUTH AND START SEEKING CHANGE

Narcissism isn't like a hiccup. It's not going to go away if you give it enough time. A narcissist will continue to manipulate, hurt, confuse, abuse, control, and take advantage of you for as long as possible. Unfortunately, you don't have "as long as possible" to decide whether you would like to step out of the relationship and create a better life for yourself.

You need to decide now.

A Coping Mechanism

There is no denying that narcissism is a harmful psychological phenomenon. But we can't simply call it "bad" and leave it at that. All the harmful effects of narcissism are real. Narcissists can physically, mentally, and emotionally abuse their victims.

However, it is also important to know the "why."

In many cases, NPD is merely a coping mechanism. We had earlier understood what trauma-associated narcissistic symptoms or TANS was all about. But here is something surprising. Research has shown that some medical experts find it difficult to distinguish between TANS and post-traumatic stress disorder, or PTSD (Simon, 2002). If that is true, then many narcissists are using their condition as a defense mechanism against past trauma.

In many cases, parents use manipulative behavior on their children from a young age. We know how impressionable children can be. At a young age, they are like sponges, absorbing behavior, ideas, facts, accents, and even personalities from other people. If they constantly witness their parents manipulating them or other people, then they begin to mimic them. Eventually, the behavior becomes part of their character. If narcissists have used a behavior all their life, then it is going to be difficult to remove it from them.

Additionally, if children are overly praised for good behavior and excessively criticized for negative behaviors, then they begin to start lying to their parents in order to avoid such criticisms. If they make a mistake, then they will try to hide the mistake in order to receive praise instead of criticism.

All of the above situations cause a child to develop emotional and mental habits.

Despite the fact that we are made to focus on certain aspects of narcissism, remember that it is:

1. An external-facing coping mechanism for a feeling of self-worth or,
2. Low self-esteem that has developed through past trauma, childhood treatment, or abuse.

Now, this places people in a tough situation. Should they focus on the narcissist because of their past or should they focus on themselves first? What is the right thing to do? If they choose to take care of themselves first, are they going to be considered selfish?

Thinking about your next action should be like those situations where you are shown the safety procedures on a plane. No matter what airplane you fly in, the steward or stewardess always explain that in case of an emergency, you should put the oxygen mask over yourself first and then place it over someone else.

You have been giving them attention this whole time and despite what you do, there does not seem to be any change in their behavior. It is time to try things differently. It is time for you to take the oxygen of your life first. Besides, if you can help yourself, then you are better equipped to help the narcissist in your life if you truly do think they need help. Otherwise, you might become susceptible to the influence of the narcissist again.

As you ponder the above situation, another question might pop into your head.

Is It Possible To Live With a Narcissist?

Many times, when I come across people who ask me this question, I find that they are already aware that the standard advice is to "simply leave." However, they choose to stay. They have made up their minds to give the person another chance. Or they may truly be in love. In plenty of situations, they have children with the narcissist and while they would like to leave, they feel that they have a responsibility, "for the children." I have also come across cases where the only thing keeping the person stuck in the relationship is his or her religious beliefs.

In such situations, things become complicated. But it does not mean that they are beyond help. If you find yourself in a similar situation, then there are things that you can do as well.

Step 1: Face The Truth

Let's look at a narcissist for who they really are. This might be a difficult step for many, since they don't want to imagine negative thoughts about someone that they care about. However, as the saying goes; you can only treat a problem if you accept that there is a problem in the first place.

Narcissism is a problem. And you need to come to terms with that idea.

Look at a narcissist for who they really are.

In some cases, you might be dealing with someone who has mental health issues. The person might have experienced a dark past that has twisted his or her viewpoint. Their behavior is far from normal or harmless.

You are the victim of their actions, thoughts, words, and ideas. They know that you have feelings for them or for some reason, you stay with them. This gives them the reason they need to plant their influence on you.

Additionally, stop making excuses for your partner. It is understandable that you would like to dilute their actions and intentions. But doing so won't help you get to the problem. You are covering up for them, which further encourages them to continue with their behavior.

Do not try to think that the narcissist isn't aware of their actions. There is plenty of research and even experts understand that not only do narcissists accept who they are, but they embrace it completely (Psychology Today, 2011).

Step 2: Have Healthy Expectations

There are some things that a narcissist will never do. In other words, there are a few things that are realistically possible with a narcissist and there are things that you cannot expect from them.

They Are Never At Fault

The first thing that you should remember is that there are rare instances of a narcissist accepting blame. In the eyes of a narcissist, either they are right or they are worthless. They don't think of being wrong and taking the effort to get better. Why should they? They are perfect and exceptionally talented as they are. What is there to improve?

This lack of responsibility also extends to their behavior. If they commit a mistake, then it is the fault of everyone and everything else. Did they not cook a dish properly? The recipe is terrible. Arrived late to work? The car is acting strange (if there was no traffic to blame that day). The only things that they see are reasons that explain why they couldn't do anything the way they wanted to.

If they accept blame, then their self-esteem takes a nosedive and they feel worthless and flawed. In those situations where they know they have no excuse to provide, they want you to blame and despise them. They use that as ammunition to feel worse. Some even go so far as to say that the pressure of doing things right, in order to avoid their non-narcissistic partner from blaming or despising them, is the reason they made the mistake in the first place.

Pick Your Battles

You need to let minor jabs and insults go. They are going to happen frequently and they are aimed at getting a reaction out of you. If you do not pick your battles, then you will be in conflict for every single thing. This can be mentally exhausting to you, since you have to maneuver around a narcissist, trying to avoid hurting them too much but at the same time, letting them know that they committed a mistake. A narcissist, on the other hand, won't be exhausted by such encounters because they do what they always want to do.

Save your arguments and discussions for the serious matters. In fact, the fewer reactions you give a narcissist, the less they begin to target you with abuse.

If you have the ability to leave the relationship, then you should keep that option close to you. Sometimes, no matter how much you try, you may not be able to get through to a narcissist.

We are going to look in detail and when you should think about saying goodbye and what is the best way to do it in a later chapter.

Processing Past Fights

Narcissists won't go back to their previous fights. To them, it feels as though you are rubbing their nose in it in order to make them feel guilty.

One of the best approaches to take when you would like to talk about the past is to use the term "we" instead of "you."

Example of what you shouldn't say: Last night, what you said was very hurtful. If there was a problem, then you should have come to me. You don't need to say the things that you did.

Example of what you should say: I know that we love each other and want the best for us. It would help if we started communicating with each other more. We don't have to do it immediately. But let's find ways to talk about things that trouble us. Let's be extra mindful about how we phrase our words so that we don't end up hurting each other.

Step 3: Start Implementing Boundaries

Narcissists do not take responsibility for their words or actions. They feel that they are right all the time and when you point out something, they feel that they have the right to hit you with verbal attacks.

They don't respect your boundaries and many will go so far as to criticize your taste in things and your belief system. In such cases, you need to call out the narcissist. Now, remember that this situation is quite different from the previous step, where you are willing to ignore minor jabs, sarcastic comments, and insults. In this step, we are talking about things that you cannot let go, such as them constantly mocking your tastes and preferences, your way of life, your likes and dislikes, and so on.

Some narcissists will give you a low blow (what even is a low blow to them) by calling you terrible and disgusting names. After a while, they expect you to forget about all of that and pretend like they never said anything.

Let me explain with an example.

I knew a man named Jack (names are changed) who once found out that his wife Anna had reconnected and spent time with an ex-boyfriend while he was away on a trip. After he returned, he discovered what she had done and decided to talk to her about it. His approach was to have a conversation; to hear her side of the story first before he could come to any conclusion.

She, on the other hand, became suddenly more aggressive. "You are just jealous of his good looks. I was just doing you a favor by sleeping with you. Just accept what I do for you and leave me alone."

At that time, Jack responded by saying that Anna had crossed a boundary, had betrayed him, and that he did not want to see her ever again. This surprised Anna. She did not expect his reaction and when she realized that Jack actually meant it, she begged him to stay.

It was later discovered that Anna had reflexively reacted to Jack the way her mother had reacted to her father when she was young. She realized that she, in fact, loved Jack. After a proper discussion, she decided to go to therapy in order to better understand herself and her reactions.

When narcissists are reminded of their actions and the consequences of it when it occurs, it is like putting a mirror in front of them. They are forced to examine their actions.

Public Humiliation

In many cases, the narcissist is able to use public humiliations to their advantage. How they humiliate you depends on their frame of mind or how far they are willing to escalate the situation. For example, you could be sitting in a restaurant and the narcissists might at first begin complaining about the service, even though it is perfectly alright. To them, it does not fit a particular standard that only they are aware of and hence, it is automatically bad. They might instantly get angry, insist that the two of you should leave the restaurant and, if you try to explain to them, they might just stand up and leave on their own. Or they might yell at you in the middle of the street and start walking away from you.

You need to decide if this is something you can live with, or if you are going to draw the line. If a narcissist is capable of doing it once, then he or she is capable of repeating his or her actions again. Their reactions are the way they cope with what they think is an insult to their self-esteem.

So just how do you react?

Let's say that you are on a date, having what you think is a pleasant conversation, and you notice the other person suddenly reacts very strongly to something. For whatever reason, they got offended by what you said and simply left the restaurant. This is a maneuver to make you chase after them. They like the fact that you are capable of going after them despite what they do.

Your next step is to not make a move, no matter how good looking, charismatic, or charming the other person is. Remember that you are good-looking, charming, and charismatic yourself. And let no one tell you otherwise. Calmly sit in the restaurant and continue with your meal. You could send a text message to the person something along the lines of: "I didn't mean to offend you. Let us start over again. Why don't you come back to the restaurant and enjoy this nice dinner with me? Let us see where this evening takes us this time."

Remember that if the narcissist decides to not return, then no harm. Enjoy your evening like nothing happened. Do not contact the person again or do not even expect him or her to get in touch with you. They have crossed a boundary and they should know that they did.

What if you are in a relationship with someone? Then you use the same tactic as above. Except this time, you could then choose to send a text message such as: "Let's try and have a lovely evening."

After that, do not chase after them. In some cases, you might notice that the narcissist might react strongly after you return home. Do not interrupt. Let them finish saying what they have to and then remind them that they have crossed a boundary. You are going to refuse talking or doing things for them because of the things that they have said to you. Let them know that you mean it.

Once they realize that you have been seriously affected by what they said, they may slowly come to their senses.

Escalating Verbal Abuse to Physical Abuse

No human being should stand for physical abuse. You did not lead your life and reach where you are right now just so you can endure physical attacks on your person. The best way to prevent physical abuse from even appearing in the future is to stop the verbal abuse.

Do not give any excuse in your mind where you think that the next time, things will be better. There is no justification for verbal abuse.

Here is one example I can use from an encounter with an abuse victim.

Don was married to Angela for nearly two years. Within that time, her verbal abuse had developed into physical abuse. She hadn't yet struck him, but she would grab his arm tightly on occasions when she would be really angry.

One night, during a dinner party with friends, Angela did not like something that Don had said and proceeded to kick him underneath the table. At that time, Don had decided that he was done with Angela's behavior and yelled "ouch!" loudly. The dinner was an awkward event and Angela would throw angry looks at Don whenever she got the chance.

When they reached home, Angela immediately turned to Don, pointed a finger at his face and proceeded to yell. "Don't you ever do that again! Never ever, do you understand? I am not going to let it pass next time."

Don did not react instantly. He had come to the conclusion that Angela had crossed a boundary that she should never have. He calmly told her: "We have been married for two years and I want to genuinely believe that you did not mean to do what you just did. It is not acceptable for you to lay a hand on me or say those things that you do. If you are willing, I am ready to have a conversation about the situation and apologize if I had done something wrong."

Angela reacted strongly. In her mind, Don was at fault and she was the victim. However, Don remained calm and held his stance. Despite the fact that Angela used several excuses to make sure she blamed Don, he continued to persist. Eventually, Angela realized that her husband was being serious and agreed to have a conversation about their relationship. She realized that she had to be more careful about the way she treated him, or else their marriage would indeed end.

Never put yourself through the phase of explaining or justifying a narcissist's actions.

Verbal abuse is still abuse. Do not justify it.

Step 4: Prepare For the Pushback

As we had seen in the example above, Angela continued to blame Don for the situation. Her actions are what we commonly refer to as the pushback. You are not going to be able to get through a narcissist's defences that easily. They will retaliate and make you feel like they are the victim and you have caused them much harm. If you know that you are not the guilty party and if you hadn't done anything to cause the person any harm, then do not relent easily. Do not sacrifice your position or else they might expect you to give up on your arguments in the future as well.

In fact, even after you set boundaries, the narcissist is going to attempt to come up with his or her own demands. They are attempting to manipulate you into dropping the topic or changing your stance on the subject altogether. In fact, they might bring up past topics in order to throw you off guard.

Remember the below points when you are dealing with the situation, before or after you have established boundaries:

- Expect a pushback. Know that the person is going to use every trick in the book to throw you off-kilter. They might suddenly become verbally abusive, dredge up past mistakes, or even twist scenarios in order to match their viewpoints.
- Stay calm. I can understand that some people experience strong emotions. They simply want to explode. Others cannot wait to be done with the situation. However, do not easily give up your position. If you show the narcissist that there is a way for them to get the upper hand, they will use that in the future.
- You are not the one being unreasonable. You are not the one who had abused the person. Do not blame yourself, despite what the narcissist might say to you. You are not controlling, cruel, rude, or whatever else the narcissist decides to call you.
- Your end goal is to get the narcissist to have a conversation. Sit down so you can both establish boundaries.
- As mentioned above, even after you have created boundaries, the narcissist might attempt to cross them. Don't accept it. If they start taking your money without your permission, keep your financial resources under lock and key. Change the password on your credit card and let them know that you really mean to establish boundaries in your life. They need to adhere to relationships based on mutual respect.

Step 5: Establish a Support System

It is time to reconnect with your friends and family. If you had been distancing yourself from people before, then make sure you bring them back in your life. Only this time, make it a point to actively connect with them. Allow them to worry about you. If you have local support groups, then make sure you get together with people who share similar experiences such as yours. Reach out to a therapist and let him or her know at what stage of the abuse you are in. In other words, make sure that you have other people aware of your situation.

The reason for keeping such a support system is for two very important reasons:

- Narcissists are good at verbally agreeing with something. They might even make it seem genuine, but they are prone to changing their minds or even pretending they never heard what you said. Sometimes, they might change the conditions of the agreement, twisting your words and trying to make you believe that you had said something else.
- Narcissists do not like it when other people get involved because they lose their power. They know that the more support you have, the less power they can exert. Additionally, if you have support groups, then you have people to help you when the time comes. For example, if the narcissist continues to be verbally abusive, then you can take a break and head over to stay with your parents. Or you can inform the therapist or support group about how the narcissist has returned to his or her old ways again.

If you feel that the narcissist tends to change their minds about things, then keep the agreement between you and him or her in a written form. I know this might sound extreme, but when you have things written down, you are keeping proof of your agreement.

Remember that the narcissist is trying to gaslight you whenever he or she wants you to change your mind. You need to be firm about the kinds of behavior you are willing to accept in the relationship.

Try to learn negotiation skills. We are going to learn more about this in the coming chapter. When you are ready with the ability to negotiate, then you are able to defend your position better.

However, it is important to remember that through all of this, you need to focus on one important factor; rebuilding and reinforcing your self-esteem. If you have to, take various classes to build your self-esteem, invest time in activities or hobbies that you are good at, use affirmations or remind yourself about the good things about you, and surround yourself and spend time with people who appreciate you. Add more positive energy into your life. You will soon realize that the power of influence that the narcissist is trying to place on you is nothing but hollow attempts. They no longer have any effect on you.

Step 6: Professional Help

You have to recognize that perhaps both you and your partner may need professional help. If that is indeed the case, then you can seek out a couples or marriage counselor.

- If you are exhibiting symptoms of depression, anxiety, or any other mental health issue, then you should head into therapy yourself. Do not be hesitant about seeking professional help. There is nothing wrong with it and you have nothing to be ashamed of for trying to get better.

- Do not hold all your emotions inside. Talk to your family or close friends who are willing to help you. Use your support group if that makes you feel better. Always reach out to people if you are suffering from emotional or physical abuse. Do not be the helpless victim. Do not suffer in silence. You need to become proactive, not reactive.
- If your emotional condition is affecting your health, then get professional help. Seek out the advice of a doctor and get a regular check up.

Be aware of the cycle of abuse. It will help you understand how abuse can take place and the signs you should look out for.

Abuse: Your partner begins to get aggressive. He or she might lash out at you, belittle you, or display violent behavior. All of the reactions that he or she displays is a form of power play in an effort to establish dominance. It's like they are trying to show you who's the "boss."

Guilt: Once the abuse is over, the narcissist then tries to make you feel guilty. But they will never refer to their actions. In their eyes, they are justified in taking the actions that they did. Deep down, they are worried about the idea that they might be caught and if so, the consequences of the discovery of their abuse. Remember this well, the narcissist is only powerful if he or she knows that they are never going to get caught. This is why they make you feel guilty, so that you are kept reticent and, in many cases, afraid.

Excuses: The narcissist will then come up with excuses for their behavior. This is done so that they can rationalize their actions or words to themselves and continue to do it in the future. They are also doing it in order to avert responsibility. If they can convince themselves that they are not the cause of the situation, then they can divert the blame to you easily.

Normality: When the narcissist gains control, they are going to do everything in their power to maintain that dominance. They will also make sure that you do not leave the relationship. They know that if you do, then they are practically powerless. There are many ways the narcissist does this. They can pretend that nothing has happened or amp up their charm, lulling you into a false sense of security. They make it seem as if things are "normal." In many cases, the victims feel as though the narcissist has changed or that they are truly nice people who are forced to do the things that they do.

Fantasy: The narcissist will then spend time thinking about the abuse. He or she wants to inflict it again and they are fantasizing about how and when they will do it. They are capable of forming elaborate plans in order to ensure that not only can they abuse you, but they can get away with it.

Set-up: Finally, the narcissist turns their plan into action. They start creating a situation that they use to abuse you, followed by other situations to make you feel guilty and for them to escape blame. They might even ensure that you remain tame.

How can you tell if your relationship has entered the territory of abuse?

Use the small checklist below to confirm how abusive your relationship might be.

On your partner's attempts to belittle you, does he or she:

- Yell at you or is capable of raising his or her voice?
- Put you down or criticize you?
- Make you feel small to such a point that you are afraid

or too embarrassed to talk to your family, friends, therapist, or even your support group?
- Prevent you from seeking help?
- Transfer the blame to you for all the things that they say?
- Ignore you as a person and see you as an object, sometimes merely for sex or money?

On your partner's controlling behavior, does he or she:

- Control what you can or cannot do, or tell you where you can or cannot go?
- Limit your access to car, phone, or money, even though in some cases, the money and other belongings are yours?
- Act extremely possessive or jealous?
- Always check up on you, no matter what you are doing?
- Prevent you from seeing your family or friends?

Talking about your inner emotions and thoughts, do you:

- Avoid talking to your partner about certain topics because you fear the repercussions?
- Have a mindset where you believe that you deserve the punishment you are receiving or that the hurt you receive is justified?
- Feel that you are failing your partner or that you can't do anything right?
- Become fearful of your partner?
- Second guess your actions or begin to think that you are the one who is crazy?
- Feel helpless or emotionally numb?

FACE THE TRUTH AND START SEEKING CHANGE | 89

When it comes to the behavior or your partner, does he or she do any of the below:

- Try to destroy or has already destroyed your belongings?
- Physically hurt you or threaten to kill you or cause harm to you?
- Have an unpredictable and dangerous or bad temper?
- Threaten to take your children away from you or talk about hurting your friends or family?
- Force you to appease him or her sexually?
- Tell you that he or she will commit suicide or hurt themselsves if you leave?

Never justify physical abuse. Make a stand. Get help.

Remember Helplines

It is also important that you have the contact details of abuse helplines. Find the abuse hotline number in your country, or refer to the below:

- U.S. and Canada: 1-800-799-7233 (SAFE)
- UK: For women, call 0808 2000 247 and for men, call 0182 3334 244

We had earlier talked about how you can negotiate with a narcissist. In order to succeed in negotiations, you must first learn to communicate. Let's look more into that.

THE WINNING GUIDE TO COMMUNICATING WITH A NARCISSIST

You may or may not be in a narcissistic relationship. You might have gotten this book because you know someone who is in an abusive relationship and you want to know what you can do about it. Perhaps you have been thinking about helping your friend or family member communicate well with their partner. Or you could be the one who is attempting to communicate with a narcissistic partner.

We are going to learn how to bring about that communication effectively.

Level of Understanding

You are going to have to understand their point of view or at least make an attempt to understand. At the same time, you have to expect the fact that they are not going to understand you in return.

You will discover that your role is one of recognition, support, and acknowledgement. Expect the narcissist to think of you as some kind of aide-de-camp. It is a difficult situation to be in, but if you truly want to communicate, then you should prepare yourself mentally.

Make sure you separate the person from the condition. If they are one and the same, then you might think of going easy on them or attempting to forgive them for certain things. Evaluate their actions and reactions in a rational manner.

They are going to attempt to change your mind, change the topic, or even distract you. Remain focused on the topic of the conversation.

You should also listen more than you speak. In fact, your main aim is to listen carefully. You are going to pick out so many words and meanings that you might not have before. It is important that you are aware of them because you might understand your next steps.

Compassion is Key

This might be difficult for you to employ but remove your prejudices and discomfort. Use compassion as much as possible. Over time, the dynamics of the dialogue will begin to shift the longer you maintain at least some degree of compassion. However, compassion does not equate to weakness. You should remain firm about your requirements. You need to let the narcissist know that you are feeling a certain way because of their actions and things have to change.

Attempt to show compassion and understanding to your partner.

In time, the dynamics of dialogue will start to shift if you manage to maintain some degree of compassion while insisting on what you actually need.

Narcissists are going to require positive recognition. Watch out for their expressions and reactions. If you are not able to reach out to them, then they will most likely let you know in an obvious manner. If you start noticing that the situation is going to become tense, then start listening to them and empathize with them. Use words such as "I understand" or "I can relate to that" (if you really can) to let the narcissist know that you are not there to play judge, jury, and executioner. You are merely trying to find a solution to the problem.

Utilize Empathic Confrontation

Learn how to practice empathic confrontation: this is a powerful influencing skill that enables you to pinpoint discrepancies between what a person says and what they do. Empathic confrontation is typically practiced by therapists who listen to a client carefully and then encourage them to engage in some degree of self-analysis. The aim is to promote the generation of new ideas and solutions through confrontation that is empathic and gentle in nature.

The most essential part of an empathic confrontation is listening. Do not harbor any judgmental feelings towards the narcissist. Do not interrupt them by giving your views on the topic. What matters is their views. You have to be prepared for the fact that you might not necessarily like their views. You should also be aware of the fact that they might start giving a long lecture about the topic, showing off their knowledge about it, even though in actuality, they know very little.

When you are about to say something, try to use statements such as: "I am not saying this because I want to blame you or be critical. I am saying this to understand you so that we can both reach a conclusion today." Some narcissists might respond by saying, "And that is what I want as well. I want us to be the best of what we are right now." Or they might use similar messaging where it seems as though they truly want the best outcome. When you notice them responding in such a manner, then you should agree with them, but do not necessarily believe them. Narcissists can change their stance quickly, as though they have a mental switch that they can activate and deactivate at their command.

Then you have to see if you can get them to self-analyze. The language used goes along the lines of: "But I am concerned that the strategy you use or the behavior you employ leads to me being afraid of you. When I am afraid or fearful, I am unable to approach you, and this leads to avoidance. Eventually, your needs for companionship and understanding are never met." Then allow them to speak. What you have done here is that you have brought the spotlight on them without telling them that they have committed something horrible. You have brought their needs into the conversation, so they know what is at stake here. The final statement can be changed. You can even say, "I believe that our attempts to create a happy marriage are not successful" or "We might not be able to have a loving, trusting, and lasting relationship."

Allow them to speak afterwards. Let them think about their actions. Make sure that you are not forcing them to speak quickly. Some narcissists might not be prepared for introspection. They might stumble through their words or fail to articulate their message properly. Do not try to complete their sentences for them. That way, you might create a message that they might not have been intending to say.

For example, let's say that they are telling you about what actually went through their mind and they are struggling to articulate, "Trust me. I did not want to hurt you. What I was really trying to do was something else. I was. I don't know. It's just hard to explain. What I was really trying to do was..."

At that point, do not finish the sentence for them. Do not fill in the gaps that they are meant to fill. If you do, then they latch on to your reason and it is going to be even more difficult for you to get to the actual truth.

Understand When To Quit or Pause

Know when it's time to quit and continue the discussion on another occasion. Whenever the other person becomes nervous, aggressive or they shut down entirely, then it's time to call for a break.

If the narcissist feels offended, then you can change the topic in order to calm them down. But be prepared to return to the topic again.

If you feel that the person has become aggressive or nervous, or has shut down completely, then be ready to stop talking to them.

Do Not Be Critical

Whatever happens, do not criticize them for anything. Understand that direct criticism and attempting to change the person in a specific way will not work.

Narcissists have learned to erect a natural defence around them and if you are critical, then they can retaliate and criticize you back. Once they get into an attack position, it becomes difficult to get through to them. They are going to remain aggressive for the remainder of the conversation. They might even bring up the fact that you attacked them in future conversations. Some narcissists might use that as a reason for why the conversation failed to reach a proper conclusion. In their eyes, it cannot be their fault at all. All the fault lies with someone else.

React Accordingly

For example, never laugh at something the narcissist says until you know that they have truly cracked a joke and you are laughing about it. They like to think that they are funny, but sometimes, they use humor to hide their low self-esteem.

If they are using humor to attack themselves, then don't laugh. Or else they might think you are mocking them, which in turn gives them the ammunition to turn things against you.

Do not mention your achievements or the things that you do right. If you do, then you are going to be labeled the "know-it-all" or perfectionist while the narcissist resorts to self-blame and creating pity. For example, the narcissist might say, "Well, if you know everything, then why don't you have a solution? Are you doing this because you enjoy watching me suffer? You are so smart right? How come you are coming here to simply attack me?"

If the narcissist begins to take such a conversational path as mentioned above, then it is difficult to veer them on the right course.

Do Not Worry If A Narcissist Becomes Self-Centered

They have grown up being self-centered and they are not going to stop now just because you decided to have a proper conversation with them. They are going to try to place themselves and their emotions as much as possible and utterly disregard your responses. Do not think about it. Focus on the goal you would like to achieve.

If all else fails, then choose to keep quiet or smile when necessary. This might not put you in a good standing with a narcissist, but it might reduce the chances of them trying to attack you. Keeping quiet or maintaining a positive emotion will prevent you from displaying your true emotions inside. For example, if a narcissist finds out that you get agitated whenever they attack you, then they are going to increase the frequency of their attacks. They are always watchful about the reactions that their words can create in you.

Be Prepared For Anything

The understanding you have about the narcissist is your strength. Do not be naive into thinking that they have changed their minds, or they understand you. Actions, after all, communicate much better than words.

If the narcissist is able to change his or her behavior, then that can be considered as a small success. I say small success because the narcissist can relapse. You should understand that change is a long-term process. Make sure your expectations are realistic. Work with the narcissist to improve them.

You should also make it a point to understand that you might not get the exact results that you would like to achieve. Nothing follows a linear path. Results may vary and you have to be able to recognize that. But what do you do if the result is not what you were looking for? You examine the overall picture:

- Has the narcissist stopped abusing you? Is he or she reducing the number of times situations of abuse occur and if so, does it look like the only reason they are doing so is to make you feel comfortable?
- Are you allowed to go and visit friends or family? Do you have the freedom to socialize?
- Are they willing to go into therapy?
- Have they stopped abusing the freedom you have given them? Have they stopped crossing boundaries?
- What other changes have they brought into their behavior that is beneficial to you?

Remember that reduction in the frequency of actions is not the same as stopping it entirely. Less abuse is still abuse. The idea is that abuse should not happen. It should end completely.

However, given that the narcissist is making attempts to change themselves, there are some things you can allow in the name of progress and some things you absolutely cannot accept.

Create a "red line," or something that can't be crossed. You can allow them to retort in anger or make sarcastic comments if you are okay with it. But that is the extent to which they think they can get away with a strong reaction. Do not, at any moment, give them any more leeway than is absolutely necessary. If your partner had been physically abusing you or if his or her emotional abuse was scathing and hurtful, then do not give them any leeway at all. Don't even accept small remarks and sarcasm.

A narcissist can cause you stress or even choose to ignore you completely. Take a break when that happens.

Finally, make sure that you deal with a situation as and when it happens. If you hold on to a situation and decide to talk to a narcissist later about it, then they will think that you are plotting something against them. Communication is the key.

I would like to tell you that things will get easier, but I won't do that. Things are always challenging when dealing with a narcissist. But remember that you should protect yourself at all times. No relationship can be considered healthy if it involves abuse. After all, you matter. You are a living and breathing person with emotions. You are capable of feeling pain, whether emotionally or physically.

Never overlook your needs.

Having said that, sometimes you might just need to heal from a codependent relationship. What can you do in that case? We are going to look at this in the next chapter.

6

HEALING FROM CODEPENDENCY IN 45 DAYS

Recovery is not easy. The memories are always going to be there. In fact, no matter how much you recover, you might find out that the emotional or physical scars that you have won't easily leave you. Being constantly reminded about the situation also does nothing to help you with the healing process.

But there are still steps you can take to kickstart the healing process.

I have given a time limit for the healing process, but it is not a fixed time. The process of overcoming codependency takes its own time and there's no universal formula for recovery. It is okay to need more or less time, don't push yourself and try to fit the framework. Do not put any degree of pressure on yourself because you want to accomplish the healing process within a particular period of time. If you feel that you are close to the 45 day mark but you haven't seen any progress, then that does not automatically mean that you are failing to make any recovery. Instead, heal in a natural and gradual way, giving yourself the extra time you need.

Make sure that you are not placing unrealistic expectations on yourself. For example, do not say that by the time you are done healing, you are going to completely forget everything about what happened to you. You might not be able to forget the memories you are trying so hard to suppress. In fact, you might start having irrational fears about the memories, reacting strongly or experiencing strong negative emotions going through you.

If you are able to forget what happened to you, then that is a wonderful result. On the other hand, if you are not able to completely forget the things that happened to you, then use your memories as learning points. Allow them to teach you valuable lessons that you can use to help yourself and perhaps even family or friends who are in a codependent relationship.

Healing results in the following traits:

- You have autonomy in your life.
- You can genuinely express yourself. You can be an authentic person without feeling guilty about it.
- You are capable of being intimate without worrying if something bad is going to happen to you.
- Feelings, emotions, thoughts, and values can be explored freely. You realize that you can create goals for yourself.

Healing usually goes through four stages.

Abstinence

This stage is necessary to distance yourself from codependency as much as possible. The main aim is to divert your attention from somebody else and focus it on yourself. In other words, your control is not based on external factors, but comes from internal will and need. You are motivated to do something because you want to do it, not because someone else is expecting you to do it. Perfect abstinence might not be possible. As I mentioned earlier, by taking the example of your memories, you might not be able to abstain from codependency. But the key point is to do the best you can.

Awareness

This is an important stage. When you are aware of your actions, thoughts, emotions, and words, you can better control them in the future. You won't allow someone else to influence them.

One of the lingering effects of codependency is denial. The more you deny, the more you are opening yourself up to accepting certain things that you should not be. Do not deny what has happened to you, no matter how difficult it is to think or talk about it, or deal with it.

Acceptance

You can only deal with a problem if you accept that there is one. Similarly, you can only heal from a situation if you accept that you were involved in that situation. Allow yourself to heal. Do not justify what has happened to you.

After all, when you resist, things persist.

Action

All of the above stages are good for recovery. But the final one might very well be the most important one. You need to start implementing measures to get out of the abusive relationship.

Don't expect others to make you happy. Make yourself happy. Say "no" to the inner critic or mindset that tries to bring you back to your old habits. Set boundaries and do not compromise on them easily.

Start taking risks. Learn more about yourself. There might be a few surprises that might just delight you.

Let us examine the steps that you need to take in order to begin the healing process.

Step 1: Be Honest With Yourself

You are the victim. Allow yourself to recognize that fact.

- What happened to you? Were you subjected to emotional abuse? Were you abused physically? Do not hide from those facts. You need to bring them from the hidden parts of your mind to your conscious self.
- Are you truly happy being in a relationship with a narcissistic person? Then tell yourself what you truly feel. Have you been holding on to your anger? Do you feel a sense of sadness threatening to overwhelm you? Are you feeling depressed or do you experience panic attacks? No matter what you are going through, recognize it without lying to yourself.
- Do not twist reality to fit a certain narrative. You are being manipulated into thinking in a certain way. Don't explain the abuser's actions. They are not your concern. Right now, your only focus is yourself.
- Stop placing your value and self-worth in the hands of someone else. Stop accepting the remarks of the abuser. Has the abuser been telling you how selfish you are? Stop thinking that way. Have you been made to think that you can be savage and heartless? Reject that notion. From this point onwards, you are only going to evaluate yourself from your perspective.
- If you start noticing that you tend to view yourself in a negative light, don't ignore your thoughts. Question why you think you are what your negative thoughts try

to describe you as. You think you are a barbarous human being? Ask yourself why? What have you done to deserve such a label? If your answer is based on the fact that you had done something that didn't fit well with the abuser's viewpoint, then tell yourself you have been manipulated to think negatively.

Be honest about how you feel. Write down your thoughts and feelings about your narcissistic relationship.

- Avoid rejecting thoughts, no matter how difficult they are. You need to face them and answer them once and for all. Sure, it won't be successful on the first try, but the more you have an answer ready, the weaker the negative thoughts are going to be. For example, if a negative thought tells you that you are weak, then don't pretend that your mind did not conjure such a thought. Ask yourself why that thought came to you. Remind yourself that you are not weak. You are a person who suffered and you are recovering. That shows strength and courage, not weakness and frailty.

Step 2: Let Out The Anger

Do you feel angry? Have you been holding on to the frustration for a long time? Have you ever felt like screaming out loud but you never get the chance?

Well, it is time you let those emotions out.

The problem with pent up emotions is that they can cause frustration, irritability, and make you feel like you don't have any control over yourself. They can be debilitating in the long term and are capable of sapping away any confidence you might have left. Bruce Lee is popularly known for saying that if you want to refill the cup, then you have to empty it first.

The same goes for your mind. Do you want to fill it with confidence, joy, hope, love, selflessness, compassion, and empathy? Then you need to empty those things that are already occupying your mind. You need to remove the self-pity, anger, sadness, blame, and all the pent-up negative energy you have been holding on to. It is time to dust out the attic of your mind and remove the junk that has been accumulating there.

Cry, shout, talk to your family or friend and tell them how you feel or what you have gone through. I once knew a victim recovering from codependency who would bring out his frustrations on a blank canvas. He would take the paint and simply strike the canvas with abstract colors. A woman who had exited from a codependent relationship would head to the gym and sweat herself out until her mind would be calm.

Once you are able to deal with the massive emotional load on your mind, you are ready to evaluate things better.

Step 3: Do Not Take Things Personally

Narcissism is a problem that the other person is dealing with. Even though you are the target of their abuse, you are not the reason for their abusive behavior.

Narcissists are reacting to trauma. If it is not you, then they will target anyone in their immediate vicinity. Just because they are acting positively towards someone does not mean that they like that person. They are probably thinking of the many ways that they can manipulate that person. Which is why, don't take what they do personally, even though it is not going to be easy.

Evaluate the situation and examine all the things that your partner has said or done. Realize that they are facing low self-esteem, emotional abuse, an unhappy childhood, or even parents who neglected them. They do not know how to deal with their past trauma and abuse. Their narcissistic personalities are their way of making sense of their reality and dealing with it.

Step 4: Improve Your Self-Worth

Positive reinforcement breeds positive reinforcement. Which is why you need to improve your self-worth. But it is easier said than done. How can one put such improvements into action?

Let's take a look at, and understand what self-worth really is.

Self-worth is often interchangeably used with self-value. Both terms have the same meaning; you value yourself and consider yourself a good person who is deserving of the respect of your family, friends, peers, and the general public. Self-worth is not just how you feel about yourself, but how you choose to act when it comes to your desires, interests, motivations, and goals.

There are many things that decide your self-worth. But rather than go through an extensive list, I am going to show the factors that **do not** reflect your self-worth.

Social Media

It really does not matter how many likes you can garner on a cool picture or how many comments flood your Instagram feed. It can be quite informative to consider the opinions of others and feel good about the fact that you have something interesting to show them. Just because the number of reactions on your social media profiles goes low, it does not automatically mean that you have low self-worth. Those things are not mutually exclusive.

Goals

It is great to achieve your goals. But they don't decide your self-worth. There are many reasons why you can or cannot achieve your goals, from financial situations to your level of experience.

Age

Everyone grows old. But some grow old gracefully while others are always catching their reflection and ponder what they should improve or change. Remember this motto: you are not too old or too young for anything.

Body

Having a six pack is good. But it does not mean that your self-worth is automatically boosted because of that six pack. Running for five miles without breaking a sweat is healthy. But once again, the skill is not an indication of your self-worth.

Grades

We all have different skills and weaknesses. Some of us are not cut out for academic excellence. But that does not mean we are without skills or that we are not smart. A student who can get straight-As has the same level of worthiness as a student who got a F.

Friends

Remember, it is not the quantity of friends that is important, but their qualities. Your Facebook can say that you have close to 2,500 friends and that is an impressive number. But that's all that is. An impressive number. You can never say that you have an impressive collection of friends. After all, who among your friend list actually considers you as a friend?

It is not the quantity, but the quality of your friends that matter.

Money (or lack thereof)

Some days, you are going to feel like Bruce Wayne. Other times, you are going to think twice before asking for extra ketchup at your local fast food joint.

But that is okay. Life is not a single event that follows only one path. It flops and meanders, takes turns and twists in unpredictable ways. That's all there is to it. Life happens. When it is in your favor, you have money and when it is not, you lose money.

Just don't measure your self-worth based on the number in your bank account.

Likes (or Dislikes)

It does not matter if you think Die Hard is a Christmas movie and all your friends are looking at you oddly. You like something. Period. There is nothing in your likes and dislikes to use as a yardstick for your self-worth.

Other People

Now we get to the core of the matter. No one can decide your self-worth. Not even the narcissist and abuser in your life. You are the only one who can confidently evaluate yourself. Sure, your views on yourself might be twisted because of the narcissist who has been influencing you constantly.

Remember that a narcissist can use any or all of the above factors to lower your feeling of self-worth. For example, they might point out your financial situation and make you feel bad about the fact that you can't afford anything. They might even blame their troubles on the fact that you do not have enough money. If you have been attaching your self-worth to money, then their statements can dig deep into your psyche and raise negative ideas about yourself.

Step 5: Set Healthy Boundaries

One of the most important questions that people ask is just how can one set healthy boundaries? There are several ways.

Know Your Limits

Understand what your physical and emotional limits are. For example, let's say that you have come home from a long day at work and your narcissistic partner suddenly has an outburst. He or she starts accusing you of things that you are not aware of. You should let your partner know that you are exhausted and that you need some time to settle your mind. Once you are ready, you and your partner can have a proper conversation. Be firm on your decision and do not relent easily. Some narcissists are capable of throwing a tantrum, but do not allow it to affect you easily.

Remember that if you are recovering from abuse, then your decision should not accept abuse at all. Your limit should not show tolerance for even slight emotional or physical abuse. Depending on the situation, an adult throwing a child-like tantrum can be a form of emotional abuse.

Be Direct

With certain people, maintaining healthy boundaries might require you to take an indirect dialogue. Being forward with them might not be the wisest course of action. It is okay to have a long conversation about boundaries with people.

However, when it comes to narcissists and abusers, you should never leave things for interpretation. Give them the direct version of your boundaries. Tell them what they can and cannot do. Of course, it does not mean that you have to be disrespectful. Rather, you can tell your partner as politely and respectfully as possible what actions or words cross boundaries. Even after you have attempted to make proper conversation and the narcissist reacts negatively, do not blame yourself. Their reactions are not your responsibility anymore.

Give Permission. Not to Others. But to Yourself.

Many people think that they are being disrespectful if they say no to others. They want to be a good wife, husband, or romantic partner. They are aiming to be a good child or a nice friend.

Give yourself permission to rediscover yourself.

But it is important to remember that you can still be respectful, kind, wonderful, and be considered a good person even after giving yourself the permission to do things you like.

When you tell yourself that it is okay to seek life's pleasures, you are telling everyone else, "I am a good person. I am kind to you and will be there for you. But I am not going to be taken advantage of. My time is valuable as well."

You might wonder; why should you give permission to yourself? Because when you are in a narcissistic, abusive, or codependent relationship, you have stopped giving yourself permission to do things.

Remember that if your friends truly love and care about you, they won't criticize you or make you feel bad about your choices. I have met people whose friends were actually the ones to tell them to make sure they do things for themselves and helped those people create meaningful boundaries.

Think About Your Past And Present

The way you were raised is going to play a huge part in the way you handle challenges and obstacles in the present. For example, if you had been playing the role of a caretaker in the past, you have learned to automatically tune into the feelings and emotions of others. This has often pushed you towards a scenario where you were drained emotionally and physically. You might have become comfortable ignoring your own needs.

Now match your past qualities with your present ones. Have you been taking care of your partner so much that you don't care about what you want? If that is the case, then are you setting up boundaries in such a way so as to include the feelings of the other person? Are you certain your boundary limits have forced you to exclude your wants and desires?

Manage Self-Care

You might have noticed therapists and medical professionals recommend physical activity and yoga. There is a genuine reason why; these activities are going to help you focus your mind better. A sedentary lifestyle causes your mind to stagnate as well.

And it is not just about physical activities. Do you take care of your hygiene properly? Are you having enough water in a day? Do you eat your meals on time?

Be Relentless in Your Pursuit of Boundaries

For a long time, you might have been relentlessly pursuing someone else's feelings and emotions. It is now time to switch focus. Once you have set your boundaries, do not sacrifice them for anything easily.

People are not mind readers. They are not going to guess

whether you have boundaries or not. Explain it to them. And then hold on to your boundaries.

Step 6: Practice Compassionate Detachment

This is an important step in the healing process. Compassionate detachment simply means that we are not attached mentally, emotionally, or even physically to the people, things, and events in our lives. This does not mean that we are heartless and beyond caring. There is a keyword we have to keep in mind; compassionate. We do care. We just don't attach ourselves to something in a way that fails to create the highest good for all.

We now have a different question to answer; what exactly is the higher good? How do we know that it is present and that our actions are contributing towards it?

Let us look at the situation with a narcissist. When you establish your boundaries and are firm in your stance about them, then the narcissist has to now try and change his or her attitude, lifestyle, communication methods, anger levels, respect, and other factors in order to accommodate your boundaries. In other words, they are going to become less narcissistic and more respectful, playing into their role of a good wife, husband, friend, parent, or anybody else in your life.

When they are, "learning the ropes" so to speak, about your boundaries, let them. Don't become lenient and extend your limitations or help the narcissist out. Don't do the learning for them. Allow them to make mistakes, learn, and improve. Rinse and repeat as many times as possible.

Why should you do this? Aren't you becoming a cold-hearted person?

Absolutely not. If you let the narcissist learn about your boundaries, then they are going to understand it better. If you help them, then they won't learn. In fact, they will use your help to manipulate you again. If they are struggling, then let them.

I would like you to think about driving or swimming. When you begin to learn those skills, or any other skills for that matter, you are obviously going to struggle in the beginning. You are going to make mistakes, but you are eager to learn and correct yourself. That is how the learning process works. Imagine if someone else does the driving or swimming for you. You are never going to get better at them. The same condition applies to a narcissistic relationship. The narcissist has to learn about your boundaries. You can definitely show them compassion and kindness, but don't become directly involved with their development. They need to learn.

Step 7: Build Self-Confidence

What do you think about pottery making? How about playing the piano? Or let's forget a skill and think of something simpler. What do you think about a nice cold beer while you are relaxing on the patio? Or what about going to see a movie with your friends? Have you heard of that new single-player action adventure video game that has come out and you have been looking forward to playing?

Think about what you like. Look at the things that make you happy. And then stop thinking.

And start doing.

The more you focus on achieving something, like a page of a book you are writing or finishing a solo of your guitar, the more confident you are going to get about yourself. When you accomplish something, even in small ways, you feel like you are not a failure. You begin to slowly remove those negative thoughts you have about yourself. In their place will be memories of the things you got done.

Step 8: Seek Out Therapy

Some emotional needs are complex. You may not understand them or know what to do with them.

When you want to love and accept yourself, you are going to find that it might be difficult to do so. After all, you have spent most of your time loving and accepting someone else. When you look at yourself, you see a stranger. And that thought can be quite disorienting. But don't worry. There is nothing wrong with that. Your mind needs to re-caliber itself. It's like the software on your device has stopped functioning properly and you are reinstalling it.

However, that software is not going to install by itself. Someone has to do it.

In your case, that someone is your therapist. He or she understands your condition because he or she has dealt with similar conditions many times in the past.

It doesn't matter if you want to clear your mind so you can figure out next steps, remove depression, find solutions for your anxiety, or attempt to understand past wounds, get a therapist if you are finding it difficult to deal with things on your own.

Step 9: The Big "No"

Have you watched the movie *Rise of the Planet of the Apes*?

I once knew someone who had come seeking advice and after I had helped him out, he said something truly interesting. You see, in the movie, the apes are being abused by the "caretaker" of the animal pen they've been placed in. He uses an electrical prod to gleefully inflict pain and then chuckles with amusement at their reactions. There comes a time when the caretaker enters the ape enclosure and starts threatening the main ape character of the movie, Caesar. He hits the ape repeatedly with the electric prod, throwing verbal abuse at him. He tells the ape to return to his cage, snarling and threatening the primate. The scene is quite difficult to watch. However, what happens next is a moment of pure cinematic brilliance.

When the caretaker lifts his hand for one more blow, Caesar grabs his arm, puffs his chest up, stands up tall, looks down menacingly and shouts "NO!"

The man, who described this analogy to me, shared that when he first said no, it felt like the scene in the movie. Of course, he did not do it threateningly or intimidatingly. He said it in a more polite and understanding manner. But he went on to tell me that, for the first time, he felt like he had done something of his own choice. He also told me that he felt powerful at that moment.

In an abusive relationship, the abuser takes away the power from the victim. They know that if they give power, then the victim can realize that they don't have to take the abuse anymore.

This is why you have to grow comfortable with saying no. It does not matter if you have to say no to the same thing over and over again. If you don't like something, then don't sacrifice your stance and go ahead with what the abuser recommends or wants.

Step 10: Grow Your Independence

Time to step out of your shell. Start doing things on your own. If you find that some things are challenging, do not let them get you down. Instead, enjoy the process and take reward in the fact that you are doing something to improve yourself.

But how can you grow your independence?

Here are a few things you can do.

Challenge Your Beliefs and Assumptions

Some or many of your beliefs might have developed because of the abuser or narcissist. In which case, they are not your beliefs, but those of the narcissist.

Start questioning the beliefs that you have.

For example, let's say that you believe that you have to do everything in your power to make the other person happy. Ask yourself how you came to that conclusion. Why do you have that belief? Why are you neglecting your own welfare over the welfare of others? Did you always think this way?

Remember that evolution cannot be possible without change. And what you are going through is an evolution of the self. You are shedding your old personality and getting accustomed to a new version of yourself.

Make Your Own Decisions

When you start making decisions by yourself, the situation is going to seem pretty frightening. After all, you are taking responsibility for your own decisions. It is quite scary. What if you do something wrong? What if you make a mistake?

Step outside. Be yourself. Build your confidence.

But that is the beauty of it. There is something liberating about the fact that you can decide and make mistakes. You can be wrong, not because someone else said so, but because you, yourself, realized it was a mistake. The best part is that each learning experience makes you feel that much better about yourself. You grow more confident, step by step. You are okay with being wrong because someone else did not make you feel wrong; you took the initiative and your own independence to decide that you are wrong.

Probably for the first time after a long time, you will be happy being wrong!

Stop Asking Permission

You might have been used to asking for permission to do almost anything in your life. But now, you have the freedom to do it.

When I say that you should stop asking for permission, I also mean that you should stop notifying the narcissist about what you are doing. He or she is not your boss.

Be bold enough to take a step outside your home and spend time with your family or friends. Did you have a curfew, where you had to return before a particular time? Ask yourself if that curfew made any sense. Is your neighborhood dangerous? After analyzing, if you realize that there is nothing wrong with staying out late and that the only reason you were returning home early was because of the narcissist's demands, then break the rule and stay out longer.

The above example is just one of many ways you can start taking control of your life and looking for "permission."

You might think to yourself, "All I am doing is letting the person know that I am doing something. What is wrong with that?"

When you feel obligated to tell the narcissist about your actions, then you are seeking their permission subconsciously. Think of the many ways that you inform the person before doing anything. Do you text the person about your activities? Do you seek confirmation when you have to head to the gym?

Stop doing that.

7

WHEN IS IT TIME TO SAY GOODBYE

Saying goodbye is not so easy. But sometimes, that is the only option left to you. But for most victims, it is difficult to say goodbye not because they like the relationship that they are in, but because they have gotten used to it so much that they can't imagine living without it.

But recovery is not an express train. It is a slow locomotive that has many stops to make before it reaches its destination.

You need to slowly build yourself, regain your confidence and your freedom, and be able to say goodbye when the situation does not provide any easy solutions or answers.

Sometimes, even the best of intentions will be insufficient to enable the establishment of a healthy relationship with a narcissist. In such instances, individuals will have to make the difficult decision to move forward without someone abusive and toxic in their lives.

If you have chosen to say goodbye, then you need to be aware of the situation, how it could develop and the challenges you are going to face.

The Stockholm Syndrome of Relationships

Living with a narcissist or an abusive partner is like having Stockholm Syndrome. You become attached to the person who is causing you the pain and suffering. It does not happen immediately. We have seen how narcissists can isolate you from your family and friends and make you dependent on them. Eventually, you start to feel as though life has more meaning with them.

This is not you deciding your own volition. It is your mind trying to minimize mental stress and damage by seeking comfort wherever and whenever it can. And it can be quite dangerous.

Narcissistic Trauma Bonding

When a situation that is starkly similar to Stockholm Syndrome takes place in your relationship with a narcissist, then the situation is called a narcissistic trauma bonding. Humans are generally wired to create emotional bonds with the people who enter their lives. This ability and desire to bond is what connects families, friends, and other people to each other. When we feel alone, insecure, or endangered, then we seek our companionship. We look out for meaning in our lives through the bonds that we create with others.

But what happens when we bond with someone one who is capable of abusing and mistreating us? What does that relationship do to us? In such cases, our tendency and desire to form relationships works against us.

Usually, when someone abuses us, we walk away from that person. In some cases, we break ties with that individual once and for all. In a narcissistic trauma bonding, because you are showered with attention and love (and a lot of it in most cases), you begin to develop genuine feelings towards the other person.

Those feelings trap you inside that relationship, despite how bad things get. Your mind creates justifications and reasons to continue with the relationship. After all, at one point, things felt good.

The fact that you have gotten used to the relationship is also why you cannot let go of the relationship easily. All of a sudden, by saying goodbye, you are stepping out into the unknown. There is so much to learn and understand by yourself.

But there are other things that will stop you from saying goodbye, most notable, the fact that the narcissist will react. They could react in any or all of the following ways.

Begging

When the narcissist realizes that you do intend to leave, they suddenly begin to take you seriously. In their eyes, all the control and power they had is now about to crumble. They had someone who was able to stick with them through all the tough times and they thought that it would last forever. They would never have imagined that you would leave.

Earlier, they could choose to abuse you and you would comply. They would be secure in the knowledge that if something happens in the future, then all they have to do is abuse you again. If it has worked all the time, then it will definitely work again right?

Wrong. Now you are wiser. You have learned to say no.

All of their tactics become useless. They realize that there is only one thing left for them to do. Beg.

Remember that when narcissists beg, they may not be doing it out of genuine guilt. They are still thinking through all the options in their mind. There might be an option in their mind that says that they only have to beg now and when you are back in their life, they will learn to control you better.

Pleading

Some narcissists do not like to be abandoned. This is because of past trauma. They see you leaving and they feel that history is repeating itself.

If you have tried everything possible to make things better with them and they continue to abuse you, then you might have decided to end the relationship. At that point, they realize that not even begging can help. Their source of narcissistic supply is just going to walk out that door.

They then choose to change their begging tactics to downright pleading. They may apologize for all the things that they have done to you. In fact, they might apologize for things that don't need an apology. I have seen some people tell me that their narcissistic partners brought up incidents that they were not even aware of.

For example, a woman told me how her narcissistic husband, when she was about to leave him, began to plead for her to stay. He suddenly admitted to cheating on her when she was away once in the past, talking about how he had not done it again because he loved her. It was as though the act of not continuing to cheat is an indication of why the woman should stay.

Bargaining

Sometimes, narcissists will try to offer you something in order to make you stay. For example, they might mention talking about the relationship and having a proper conversation about things. They may even recommend or agree to therapy and "figuring things out." All the suggestions that they would not have considered before are actions that they are willing to take.

However, when they begin bargaining, it is important to know that they are still manipulating the situation. They are bargaining because they think that they have something that will change your mind. They are hoping to entice you back into their sphere of influence by offering you something you might have been hoping to get.

Threats and Aggression

When all else fails or if they feel like it, then narcissists employ a method known as narcissistic rage, which combines aggression, threats, or intense anger. When you decide to leave, your actions shatter their sense of entitlement, illusions of grandeur, and feelings of superiority. All of a sudden, they feel vulnerable, ashamed, and even inadequate. These are feelings that they never experienced before. They are used to being in control, acting calm, being dominating, and showcasing their power.

The difference between normal anger and narcissistic rage is that the rage is usually unreasonable, scathingly aggressive, and disproportional. Your actions have caused a deep blow to their idealized and superficial self-image.

Narcissistic rage serves two purposes. On the outside, it is a manipulative tool. It uses fear and intimidation to get you to do something. The narcissist thinks that if he or she is aggressive enough, you will be too afraid to do anything against their wishes.

On the inside, it is a pain-avoidance tool. They are hurt and they want to cover that pain through rage. After all, if they admit that they are hurt and begin to tend to their wounds, it might make them look weak. And that is something that they do not want to do.

Think of a spoiled child in a toy store. If you tell the child that you are not going to get a toy, what do you think happens? The child might throw a tantrum. Narcissistic rage is a form of tantrum, but to the victim, it can feel intimidating. You, as a victim, were intimidated by many things that the narcissist used to do. All of a sudden, you are faced with pure anger and rage. It can be quite scary. You might be tempted to abandon your plan. But remember that the narcissist is actually afraid of you. He or she fears your actions and in that, you need to be sure of yourself.

Do not allow yourself to be easily affected by a narcissist's emotions. You have to keep reminding yourself that they are reacting out of self-interest.

No Contact Rule

Once you have bid your farewells and are now working to become independent, don't think that the narcissist won't attempt to get in touch with you.

You have to establish a "no contact" rule where you are not going to entertain the narcissist's attempts to contact you. Get into therapy if you like. Live with friends or family. Try to form new friendships and invite people into your life. The trick is to form positive bonds while getting rid of the effects of the negative bond that you were part of for so long.

Take the "no contact" period to heal. Look back at the advice and suggestions that were highlighted in the previous chapter. The narcissist might employ the tactics mentioned previously. They might try a combination of pleading and aggression. They might become relentless in their pursuit of you.

If you prefer, you can move to a location that is only known to you and a group of close friends. Additionally, try to remove your previous contact details if possible and cut off any links to the narcissist. Think of the situation like you are going to a yoga or wellness retreat. You have to let go of all the things that connect you to a world of influence. Once you are in your "no contact" zone, you are going to focus on healing. If you truly crave companionship, depend on your support group, new friends, family members, and close friends.

Detach

Detachment is the idea of being objective or becoming aloof. When you are leaving a narcissistic relationship, you need to be both objective *and* aloof.

You are going to find it difficult to accept that even after all the affection and attention that you had given to your partner, even after all the mind games you've endured and the abuses you had suffered, after the many emotional dances you had to perform, they still could not offer any real love or attention.

Worst of all, you have this sense that you just wasted so much time of your life pursuing something that was never going to yield any returns. You feel hopeless that you lost so much time in your life and, if you had it all back, you would have done something else. We are not immortals. We don't have all the time in the world to recuperate.

Our lives are limited. Being with a narcissist has made it even more limited. And now, you have to spend even more time in a healing process. All of that disappointment can be crushing.

But that is why you are not going to waste any more time. You are going to accept the fact that some people are just not capable of returning the love, compassion, and attention that was so generously poured into their lives.

And that is why, you are going to detach yourself from the narcissist.

You are going to become aloof from the narcissistic influence in your life and have an objective overview of your situation. Detachment occurs in several stages.

Stage One

You are going to start by refusing to take blame for all the things that happened to the narcissist. You are going to refuse blaming yourself for many things that happened in your relationship. You are finally seeing things in the way that they should be seen. All this time, you had a filter that you would use to justify the narcissist's behavior. Once that filter comes off, then you see the situation for what it really is; a person using another person for his or her own twisted goals.

Stage Two

When you start examining things objectively, you start feeling anger and resentment. Do note that you may still harbor feelings for your partner, but some things have changed. For example:

- You know when your partner is lying to you and those lies don't affect you anymore.
- If your partner tries to manipulate you, then you become indifferent to his or her efforts.
- You start to imagine a life where you are not bound by so many restrictions, abuses, fear, hate, and rules.
- You begin to feel good about who you are as a person.

Stage Three

In this stage, the focus turns to you. Once you have gained awareness, you begin to question so many things in your relationship. You might start researching online about what to do and if there are other people going through the same thing that you are. Support groups and your friends are going to be your goals since you want to have people in your life who can help you free yourself from the present situation.

When you are in stage three, you are going to notice...

- Whenever you see the narcissist in your life, you are filled with disgust and perhaps even loathing.
- You begin to question how you could have loved the person in the first place. All the love and affection that you had garnered for the person has now left your system.
- You begin to react even when he or she so much as does even the smallest thing that could be construed as out of line.
- You begin to "break rules." You start doing things outside the relationship. You realize that not everything you have to do should be connected to your partner.
- You begin to make plans or preparations to leave the relationship or find ways to end it.

Stage Four

This is the final stage of the detachment process. At this point, you are ready to end the relationship. In some cases, the victim might not even care whether he or she has made plans to depart from the relationship. They just want to get away and they do. They contact their relatives or friends and without so much as a goodbye, they leave.

When You Have Decided To Leave

This is going to be the hardest decision you are going to make, but you can do it. Once you have decided to leave, then don't look back. Do not reconsider or allow the narcissist to change your mind. If you fall back into the relationship, then you will find it even more difficult to leave the next time, since the narcissist is aware of what you will do to leave.

Allow yourself to feel everything that you may have become numb to in the past due to the abusive nature of the relationship. You don't have to stop yourself from feeling sad because of lost time or angry for all the things that you endured. Let each emotion flow through you. Think about it; you can finally react without holding back.

As Hard As a Rock

Master the grey rock method so that a narcissist no longer sees you as a target. Remember that what fuels a narcissist the most is his or her desire to be admired by others. He or she wants to be in the spotlight, which is why they strive for attention.

What happens if their supply of attention is cut off completely?

But how can you do that?

You act like a rock.

In the gray rock method, you are going to be emotionally unresponsive to the narcissist. This is useful when contact with a narcissist cannot be entirely terminated. Whenever the narcissist appears in your life, you are not going to entertain them by showing them attention. You are simply going to pretend to be oblivious to their presence. They might attempt to grab your attention by pleading, yelling, abusing, showing kindness, using threats, or even attempting to reconcile.

In some cases, you have to realize that you may not get closure or have a final conversation with the narcissist. In such cases, do not hold on to any hope of connecting. Simply leave the relationship without giving the person time to respond or even providing an explanation. After all, they had plenty of time to try and make amends or have a conversation. From that point onwards, it does not matter if they truly want to have a conversation or if their intentions are genuine.

It is over.

During your turbulent change, you need love and support. Join a support group, make new friends, connect with your family or old friends. Find positive reinforcements and surround yourself with genuine warmth and compassion. The more you receive honest care, support, and love, the faster you are able to let go of whatever constituted for love in the narcissistic relationship.

Eventually, the uncertainty and pain will slowly subside. You will begin to enjoy your newfound freedom.

The Game of Gossip And Other Tactics

Be prepared for the narcissist to start using underhanded methods in order to get you back. They may gossip about you or slander your name to your family and friends. They want to create a bridge between you and the people you care about. That way, they hope that you become alienated and then turn to them for support.

They might attempt to use a technique known as "hoovering." You are leading your life free from your narcissist partner's influence. One night, you receive a text on your phone or your Facebook. It says, "I am in such a bad place right now. I don't know what to do. I need help."

Sometimes, you might see other sentences added to the message such as, "You are the only one I could turn to" or "You were right all along, and I should have listened."

You want to completely ignore the message, but you feel some sense of pity, Your good nature takes over. Your sense of empathy and compassion blast their way into your consciousness. You send a quick reply, thinking that perhaps it will end the situation completely. You say, "What do you want? Stop bothering me."

You have fallen for a trap. You have been hoovered.

Now your life is just waiting to be disrupted again. The narcissist will become even more persistent, sending you texts filled with remorse. He or she will try to reach out to your good side.

All of the above tactics might be used by the narcissist.

Before you fall prey to such tactics, here are some things that you should do.

Explain Your Story

Get in touch with your friends and family and explain to them the entire situation. Tell them the kind of relationship you were part of. Talk to your therapist and support group and let them know the kind of person your narcissistic partner was. Now you have people on your side and they are ready to retaliate in case the narcissist contacts them.

Be Aware of Hoovering

No matter how desperate things may seem, you are not responsible for the narcissist. Their actions are their responsibility. Not yours. If you see text messages or other communication methods being used to get in touch with you, ignore them. Don't even respond with an insult or snide remark.

Change Contact Details

We had earlier seen how you can change contact details in order to cut the narcissist from your life completely. Do it. And once you have done it, don't look back.

Focus More On Yourself

The more you take care of yourself, the less time you have for the narcissist. In the previous chapter, we saw how you can recover by doing the things that you like. Learn to nurture yourself more.

Emergency

Keep emergency contact numbers with you at all times, if necessary. It is far better to be prepared than be taken off-guard and have no options to resort to.

I would be incredibly thankful if you could take just 60 seconds to write a brief review on Amazon, even if it's just a few sentences!

YOUR OPINION MATTERS

SCAN ME TO LEAVE A QUICK REVIEW

Scan me

CONCLUSION

One thing I like to say to people is that they should not use the information provided in this book to diagnose people they know. For example, let us say that you know a friend who has a partner who engages in love bombing. He or she showers so much affection on your friend. Do not automatically assume that the partner is a narcissist. Perhaps the partner truly loves your friend. Perhaps he or she has never found someone like your friend. The partner is trying to figure out the best way to show love and affection to your friend. In fact, I like to think that many people engage in love bombing when they first enter a relationship. It's like a magical moment in their lives. The constant text messages, late night conversations, and movie times are just the couple's way of understanding each other and enjoying each other's company.

Imagine what would happen if you were to suddenly go to your friend and suggest that their partner could be a narcissist. It might destroy something good.

Having said that, I also like to say that you are a human being with a collection of wants, desires, hopes, dreams, and goals.

You were not placed here on this rock floating in space around a big ball of fire just to be controlled by someone else.

You need to take care of yourself. Your life is valuable and you deserve love, respect, kindness, joy, positive relationships, and all the good things that others receive.

When you enter a narcissistic relationship, you suddenly find yourself devoid of all the things that make you who you are. Your ambitions? They don't matter anymore. Your likes and dislikes? They are not your concern. The freedom you had once when you could make important life decisions by yourself? Well, there exists no more freedom.

Suddenly, you find yourself truly unhappy. And even though you are unhappy, you cannot free yourself from that unhappiness. In some cases, you have responsibilities or you are dependent on something. You and your partner may have children, you may enjoy certain lifestyle benefits, or you may lack resources.

Your family and friends may be urging you to leave, but that suggestion makes you feel ashamed of yourself. After all, you feel like since you got yourself into this mess, you deserve it.

That is not true. Everyone makes mistakes. Your only mistake was that you chose to love someone wholeheartedly. You decided to give your attention and respect to someone. And they took all of that and turned them into something grotesque.

What is wrong in giving love? Sacrificing the things in your life for someone else is noble. It shows your good nature and your pure heart.

At this point you should not feel ashamed. In fact, you are probably experiencing the feeling of shame because of the narcissist.

And for that reason, you are going to start taking steps to better your situation. Whether you choose to leave or to talk it out, remember that your needs and desires are important. Be confident. Stand your ground. Reject further abuse or manipulation.

It is time for you to deal with a narcissistic personality and escape from your codependent relationship.

Are you Being Mind-Controlled by a Narcissist?
Find out if you are and learn how to escape it right now!

To receive your FREE guide visit the link:

https://helenbooks.activehosted.com/f/3

OR

REFERENCES

Ambardar, S. (2018). What are the DSM-5 diagnostic criteria for narcissistic personality disorder (NPD)?. Retrieved 13 March 2020, from https://www.medscape.com/answers/1519417-101764/what-are-the-dsm-5-diagnostic-criteria-for-narcissistic-personality-disorder-npd

Bree, B. (2018). Narcissistic Abuse Affects Over 158 Million People in the U.S. Retrieved 22 February 2020, from https://psychcentral.com/lib/narcissistic-abuse-affects-over-158-million-people-in-the-u-s/

Chow, D. (2013). Narcissists' Lack of Empathy Detected in Brain Scans. Retrieved 13 March 2020, from https://www.livescience.com/37684-narcissistic-personality-disorder-brain-structure.html

Huang, Y., Kotov, R., de Girolamo, G., Preti, A., Angermeyer, M., & Benjet, C. et al. (2009). DSM–IV personality disorders in the WHO World Mental Health Surveys. British Journal Of Psychiatry, 195(1), 46-53. doi: 10.1192/bjp.bp.108.058552

Luo, Y., Cai, H., & Song, H. (2014). A Behavioral Genetic Study of Intrapersonal and Interpersonal Dimensions of Narcissism. Plos ONE, 9(4), e93403. doi: 10.1371/journal.pone.0093403

Psychology Today. (2011). Do Narcissists Know They Are Narcissists?. Retrieved 1 March 2020, from https://www.psychologytoday.com/us/blog/beautiful-minds/201103/do-narcissists-know-they-are-narcissists

Zajenkowski, M., Maciantowicz, O., Szymaniak, K., & Urban, P. (2018). Vulnerable and Grandiose Narcissism Are Differentially Associated With Ability and Trait Emotional Intelligence. Frontiers In Psychology, 9. doi: 10.3389/fpsyg.2018.01606

Made in United States
Orlando, FL
01 August 2024